Contributions to Economics

For further volumes:
http://www.springer.com/1431-1933

Daniela Vandone

Consumer Credit in Europe

Risks and Opportunities of a Dynamic Industry

Physica-Verlag

Professor Daniela Vandone
Università degli Studi di Milano
Department of Economics, Business and Statistics
Via Conservatorio 7
20122 Milan, Italy
daniela.vandone@unimi.it

ISSN 1431-1933
ISBN 978-3-7908-2100-0   e-ISBN 978-3-7908-2101-7
DOI: 10.1007/978-3-7908-2101-7
Springer Dordrecht Heidelberg London New York

Library of Congress Control Number: 2009926005

© Springer-Verlag Berlin Heidelberg 2009
This work is subject to copyright. All rights are reserved, whether the whole or part of the material is concerned, specifically the rights of translation, reprinting, reuse of illustrations, recitation, broadcasting, reproduction on microfilm or in any other way, and storage in data banks. Duplication of this publication or parts thereof is permitted only under the provisions of the German Copyright Law of September 9, 1965, in its current version, and permission for use must always be obtained from Springer. Violations are liable to prosecution under the German Copyright Law.
The use of general descriptive names, registered names, trademarks, etc. in this publication does not imply, even in the absence of a specific statement, that such names are exempt from the relevant protective laws and regulations and therefore free for general use.

Cover design: WMXDesign GmbH, Heidelberg

Printed on acid-free paper

Physica-Verlag is a brand of Springer-Verlag Berlin Heidelberg

Springer-Verlag is a part of Springer Science+Business Media (www.springer.com)

"If you can keep your head when all about you
Are losing theirs and blaming it on you,
If you can trust yourself when all men doubt you
But make allowance for their doubting too
...
Yours is the Earth and everything that's in it
And – which is more – you'll be a Man, my son!"
[Kipling, 1895]

To Benedetta and Ludovica, my precious daughters

Acknowledgements

I wish to express my gratitude to two anonymous referees for their helpful comments, suggestions and insights. I also benefited from discussions with seminar and conference participants during various stages of the research. My thanks also to Barbara Fees for her excellent editorial assistance at Springer and to Justin Rainey for his help in preparing the English version of the work. Naturally, the usual disclaimer applies to any errors or omissions.

The research presented in this book has benefited from contributions made by the University of Milan and the Ministry of Education, University and Research, Research Project of National Interest 2007.

Contents

Introduction 1
1 Structure of the Book 2
2 Main Findings 4

1 The Determinants of Consumer Credit: A Review of the Literature 7
  1.1 Introduction 7
  1.2 The Life-Cycle and Permanent Income Theories 8
      1.2.1 Credit Demand Factors 9
      1.2.2 Credit Supply Factors 11
  1.3 Empirical Findings 12
      1.3.1 Participation in the Credit Market 12
      1.3.2 Level of Borrowing 16
      1.3.3 Cross-Country Analyses 16
      1.3.4 Over-Indebtedness 17
      1.3.5 Credit Constraints 18
  1.4 Behavioural Economics 19
  1.5 Summary of the Determinants of the Demand for and Supply of Consumer Credit 21

2 Household Consumer Credit Demand 23
  2.1 Introduction 23
  2.2 Consumer Credit in Europe 23
      2.2.1 The Diffusion of Consumer Credit 24
      2.2.2 Consumer Credit Growth Rates 29
      2.2.3 Heterogeneous Markets: Possible Causes 30
  2.3 Characteristics of Indebted Households 32
      2.3.1 The Purpose of the Analysis 33
      2.3.2 Results and Remarks 36
  Appendix 43

3 The Profitability of the Consumer Credit Industry 45
- 3.1 Introduction 45
- 3.2 The Consumer Credit Industry: Main Features 46
  - 3.2.1 Consumer Credit Lenders 46
  - 3.2.2 Consumer Credit Products 47
- 3.3. Profitability Analysis of a Sample of Specialised Consumer Credit Companies 52
  - 3.3.1 Objectives and Methodology 52
  - 3.3.2 The Sample 53
  - 3.3.3 Main Results 55
- Appendix 64

4 From Indebtedness to Over-Indebtedness 69
- 4.1 Introduction 69
- 4.2 Over-Indebtedness: Defining Features 69
  - 4.2.1 Measuring Over-Indebtedness 71
  - 4.2.2 Possible Causes of Over-Indebtedness 73
- 4.3 Policy Measures for the Prevention and Management of Over-Indebtedness 75
  - 4.3.1 Financial Education 81
  - 4.3.2 Debt Counselling Agencies 84
  - 4.3.3 Credit Bureau 85
  - 4.3.4 Transparent Information 87
  - 4.3.5 Responsible Arrears Management 88
  - 4.3.6 Interest Rate Ceilings and Usury Laws 88
  - 4.3.7 Debt Settlement Procedures 89
- Appendix 92

5 Regulatory Framework 101
- 5.1 Introduction 101
- 5.2 The New Consumer Credit Directive 102
- 5.3 Information Requirements for Consumer Credit Agreements 104
  - 5.3.1 Advertising 105
  - 5.3.2 Pre-Contractual Information 105
  - 5.3.3 Information to be Included in the Credit Agreement 110
  - 5.3.4 Information to be Provided Throughout the Duration of the Contract 110
- 5.4 Assessment of Creditworthiness 114
- 5.5 Protection of Other Consumer Rights 116
- 5.6 The Supervision of Creditors and Credit Intermediaries 119
- 5.7 Further Remarks 123
- Appendix 126

References 129

List of Tables

Table 1.1	Consumer credit demand and supply factors	9
Table 1.2	The literature of household credit	13
Table 1.3	Summary of the determinants of consumer credit	22
Table 2.1	Principal features of the three surveys	33
Table 2.2	Percentage of indebted households and average amount of exposure	36
Table 2.3	United Kingdom – Percentage of households with consumer credit in terms of socio-demographic and economic characteristics	37
Table 2.4	Italy – Percentage of households with consumer credit in terms of socio- demographic and economic characteristics	38
Table 2.5	Spain – Percentage of households with consumer credit in terms of socio-demographic and economic characteristics	39
Table 2.6	United Kingdom – Percentage of households with consumer credit in terms of financial situation	41
Table 2.7	Italy – Percentage of households with consumer credit in terms of financial situation	41
Table 2.8	Spain – Percentage of households with consumer credit in terms of financial situation	42
Table 2.9	Variables used from SHIW	43
Table 2.10	Variables used from EFF	43
Table 2.11	Variables used from BHPS	44
Table 3.1	Sample representativeness: consumer credit outstanding (millions of euros, 2006)	54
Table 3.2	Composition of the sample (millions of euros, 2006)	55
Table 3.3	The average ROA (%, 2006)	56
Table 3.4	A breakdown of the ROA (%, 2006)	57
Table 3.5	Provisions for loan losses (%, 2006)	58
Table 3.6	A breakdown of the ROA by company type (%, 2006)	60
Table 3.7	A breakdown of the ROA by country of origin (%, 2006)	61
Table 3.8	Characteristics of dependent variable and regressors	62

Table 3.9	Weighted leasted squared (WLS) estimations (dependent variable: ROA)	62
Table 3.10	Composition of the sample (millions of euros, 2006)	64
Table 3.11	Results of the one-way Anova to test for differences among the four countries: F test and significance	67
Table 3.12	Estimation of fixed effects (dependent variable: ROA)	67
Table 3.13	Estimation of random effects (dependent variable: ROA)	67
Table 4.1	Relations between possible causes of over-indebtedness and measures for its prevention and management	77
Table 4.2	Credit bureaus: benefits and costs	86
Table 4.3	Consumer insolvency regulation in EU countries	90
Table 4.4	Consumer insolvency regulation in EU countries: main contents	92
Table 5.1	Differences between the first and the new Consumer Credit Directive: information requirements	111
Table 5.2	Differences between the first and the new Consumer Credit Directive: assessment of consumer creditworthiness	115
Table 5.3	Differences between the first and the new Consumer Credit Directive: protection of other consumer rights	117
Table 5.4	Differences between the first and new Consumer Credit Directive: creditors and credit intermediaries	121
Table 5.5	Reproduction of Annex II – "Standard European Consumer Credit Information", Official Journal of the European Union, 22.5.2008	126

List of Figures

Figure 2.1	Outstanding consumer credit in EU-27 countries (billions of euros)	24
Figure 2.2	Consumer credit as a percentage of GDP (%, 2000–2006)	25
Figure 2.3	Consumer credit as a percentage of disposable income (%, 2000–2006)	27
Figure 2.4	Consumer credit as a percentage of consumption expenditure (%, 2000–2006)	28
Figure 2.5	Consumer credit average annual growth rate (%, 2000–2006)	29
Figure 2.6	Comparison of growth rates in EU-15 countries (%, 2000–2006)	30
Figure 3.1	Outstanding consumer credit by loan type (%, 2006)	48
Figure 3.2	Non-specific purchase loans as a percentage of new loans (%, 2003–2006)	49
Figure 3.3	Relation between ROA, total assets and country (2006)	59
Figure 4.1	Indicators of over-indebtedness	72
Figure 4.2	The causes of over-indebtedness	75

Introduction

The diffusion of consumer credit differs widely from country to country, although in recent years, the use of consumer credit has recorded high levels of growth throughout most of Europe. In some countries, such as the United Kingdom, Germany, Spain and France, household unsecured debt levels are high, whilst in others, such as Portugal, Italy and the new Member States of the EU, they remain comparatively contained.

These differences stem from a variety of factors, many of which idiosyncratic – such as trends in macroeconomic variables, welfare policies, efficiency of justice systems, development of informal credit markets – which have an impact on the demand for and supply of consumer credit and, consequently, the size of local credit markets.

These are flanked by others, related both to households' attitudes to thrift and indebtedness as well as the characteristics of the credit industry and the role lenders play in delivering consumer credit solutions. The extent and success lenders have in carrying out this role depends, for example, on production innovation, heightened customer service levels and operating size. These factors will dictate the extent lenders are able, firstly, to exploit economies of scale for the reduction of costs associated with lending large quantities of small-sized loans and, secondly, to build suitably diversified loan portfolios.

The developments outlined above raise important research questions from various perspectives.

Consumer credit demand is expanding throughout Europe. Why do consumers seek credit and what are their socio-demographic characteristics? Does the decision to participate in the credit market stem from the need to optimise intertemporal consumption, as traditionally posited, or does it also stem from weaknesses in borrowers' financial and economic conditions?

Consumer credit growth is not exclusively demand-driven, but is also the result of the key role played by lenders. What are the features of the European consumer credit industry across different national markets, particularly as regards lender types and credit policies? What are the profitability levels for the sector?

There is growing concern that the spread of consumer credit may also affect segments of the population most at risk of over-indebtedness. What factors transform physiological indebtedness into pathological indebtedness? What measures for the prevention and management of over-indebtedness are currently in place in Europe and how effective are they?

The recent new Directive on credit agreements for consumers introduces many new aspects in comparison to the previous regulatory scenario set by the first Directive and goes some way in establishing a common regulatory framework. How will the new Directive affect integration between European markets and the future of the consumer credit industry in general? What regulatory instruments have been adopted to ensure higher levels of consumer protection?

This book intends to provide answers to these questions by carrying out a comparative analysis of the most significant problems that characterise consumer credit in a varied European scenario.

1 Structure of the Book

The book is divided into five chapters. Chapter 1 provides an overview of the literature of household indebtedness with the aim of providing an outline of the determinants of the demand for and the supply of consumer credit, its diffusion and distribution amongst different segments of the population.

The economic models typically adopted are those within the framework of life cycle and permanent income theories, on the basis of which individuals via their decisions relating to saving and indebtedness seek to improve their welfare by intertemporal consumption smoothing. According to these models, the factors that influence the demand for and supply of consumer credit can be "individual" and "institutional". The former relate to the demographic, social and economic variables that characterise an individual or his/her household and include level of education, qualifications, family size, type of employment, income and wealth. Institutional factors are those that relate to a consumer credit market's contextual features, such as the characteristics of the justice system, the presence of information-sharing mechanisms amongst lenders, the existence of informal credit circuits (loans from family and friends).

In recent years, behavioural economics has proposed alternative theories to those adopted by Life-Cycle and Permanent Income models. This approach suggests that an individual's choices are not influenced solely by the variables mentioned above, but also by psychological factors, such as personal taste, forecasting errors and impatience. The existence of these factors leads individuals systematically to act in ways that diverge from those foreseen by the "rational choice" model of standard theories, with resulting greater risk of financial difficulties and over-indebtedness.

Chapter 2 analyses, on the basis of macroeconomic data, developments in the European consumer credit markets. Data from national household surveys carried out on a regular basis statistics institutes and National Central Banks is then used to build up a socio-demographic and economic picture of consumer credit borrowers. The aim here is to identify the possible characteristics of those who apply for credit or who are more likely to finance their consumption by debt as well as to obtain insights into the reasons for borrowing, particularly in relation to the evidence emerging from the review of the literature in Chap. 1.

The analysis focuses on three countries, each with differences in the extent and distribution of consumer credit, by using data from national household surveys: Italy – Survey of Household Income and Wealth (SHIW), Spain – Survey of Household Finances (EFF), the United Kingdom – British Household Panel Survey (BHPS).

Chapter 3 examines the consumer credit industry, its rapid expansion and the increased complexity and competitiveness such expansion has brought with it. Particular attention is placed on the impact these factors is having on the structure of economic results.

The performances, measured by ROA metrics, of a sample of French, German, Italian and Spanish consumer credit lenders are analysed in order to identify the reasons for the results and to what extent differences may be due to cross-country factors.

The intercurrent relation between ROA and potential explanatory variables is examined by using a Weighted Leasted Squared (WLS) linear regression model. The regressors were chosen to capture the principal features explaining lenders' profitability, i.e. cost structure, profitability of lending activity, diversification and size. Dummy variables were also included in the equation to account for contextual factors as determinants of cross-country differences along with dummy variables inserted in order to capture the differences in profitability existing between specialised finance companies, on one hand, and captives belonging to major retail and manufacturing groups, on the other.

Qualitative analyses of lenders' profitability are made on the basis of lender type – specialised finance company or captive – and nationality of parent company – domestic or foreign.

Chapter 4 addresses the question of over-indebtedness. The importance of the phenomenon lies, at least for the time being in Europe, not in its size, but in the fact that over-indebtedness mainly affects the economically and socially weakest members of society, with potentially high costs for the financial system and society as a whole.

The chapter analyses the problems related to measuring the phenomenon and establishes its primary causes. This is followed by an investigation of the measures adopted so far in Europe to tackle over-indebtedness. Despite the considerable cross-country differences that exist, an attempt is made-where possible-to identify the comparative effectiveness of the approaches used.

These measures are typically either preventive or curative. The former seek to influence behaviour on both the demand side (responsible borrowing) and on the supply side (responsible lending), whilst the latter are various ex post responses to default, such as debt management and restructuring schemes in the form of debt settlement procedures, which in some cases offer the possibility of cancelling part of the debt.

The book concludes in Chap. 5 with an analysis of the provisions of the new Consumer Credit Directive, passed in April 2008. In particular, it examines the changes introduced in comparison to the first (amended) Directive of 1986, and the effects these changes will have on consumer credit lenders and their relations with borrowers.

The Directive seeks to harmonise consumer credit in the European Union by focusing on a series of key areas: standard information to be used at all stages of the credit agreement, an assessment of households' creditworthiness, rights concerning credit agreements, and the regulation of creditors and credit intermediaries. The aim of this regulation and harmonisation is, on one hand, to promote cross-border activities by creating a credit market without internal frontiers and, on the other, to ensure that consumers throughout the European Union benefit from the same high levels of protection of their interests.

The chapter also shows that, although the Directive represents significant changes to the credit market of many EU Member States, in the most advanced credit markets its provisions were already part of national legislation.

2 Main Findings

In recent years the consumer credit market has recorded considerable levels of growth in most European countries. These growth rates have been particularly vibrant in some countries with comparatively immature consumer credit markets, such as in the most recent entrants to the European Union. In mature markets, such as the United Kingdom, France and Spain, where amounts borrowed in the form of consumer credit already represented a high percentage of GDP, growth rates continued to be positive, so demonstrating the increasing importance of this form of unsecured debt in these economies.

Leaving aside specifically national features, economic analysis has identified, on the basis of Life-Cycle and Permanent Income theories, certain individual factors, i.e. economic and socio-demographic, which, along with institutional factors, i.e. the institutional context in which borrowers and lenders are placed, influence the development of consumer credit.

Alongside the traditional models already mentioned, which essentially view the recourse to credit as a means of improving living standards as the primary reason underpinning the decision to participate in the credit market for broad segments of the population, empirical analysis applied to some countries – Italy, Spain and the United Kingdom – shows that for certain categories of borrowers the recourse to consumer credit is motivated not only by consumption smoothing, but also by the need to supplement current income and to manage conditions of financial difficulties.

The diffusion of consumer credit is driven not only by demand, but also by more sophisticated forms of lending. In fact, lenders in recent years have invested considerably in a business segment with high volume and potential earnings.

On one hand, lending volumes can be expected to grow as a result of changes in socio-cultural variables and new spending models that have made personal indebtedness more acceptable, albeit with cross-country differences conditioned by differing levels of market maturity.

On the other, lenders have considerable interests in stimulating this potential demand. On the basis of results obtained in the most advanced countries, incentives for developing consumer credit activities include, in addition to attractive profitability levels - which, for instance, in Spain and France, outstrip those recorded by the banking sector - further performance improvements offered, for example, by cross-selling. Choices adopted by banks and finance companies in these markets show that, more than in other segments of the credit market, competitive non price-based strategies used in the area of personal finance have been particularly successful in maintaining rising volumes and widening potential customer bases. These strategies have exploited both customer segmentation policies linked to multi-channel product distribution and the development of a range of lending products targeted (and marketed) to specific customer types.

Such growth is bound to have a positive effect both on cost structures, as economies of scale start to bear fruit, and commission-generated earnings, thanks to increasingly diversified and sophisticated products also in those countries where the consumer credit market, though still comparatively immature, continues to record strong levels of growth.

Another important factor that will inevitably affect the future of the European consumer credit industry is represented by changes in the regulatory environment: attempts to reduce market segmentation and favour growth in cross-border credit flows will not only ultimately benefit the customer, but will also increase competition, which will, in turn, lead to narrower interest margins and riskier loan portfolios for lenders.

The likelihood of increased credit risk stems inevitably from the extension of credit solutions to the near and sub-prime segments and more precisely to individuals most at risk of over-indebtedness.

The effects of household over-indebtedness should be addressed not only by the banking system, in relation to the potential worsening of credit quality levels, but also by policy makers, who will have to address the potential socio-economic repercussions of the phenomenon.

It is argued therefore that responsible lending and responsible borrowing solutions need to be designed capable of preventing ex ante unsustainable levels of indebtedness and resolving ex post repayment difficulties faced by individuals and households.

Chapter 1
The Determinants of Consumer Credit: A Review of the Literature

1.1 Introduction

The literature of consumer credit is sizeable. Such a body of work reflects not only the composite nature of unsecured debt, but also the fact that different methodological approaches exist depending on the research questions under analysis and the objectives sought.

Four main approaches can be seen: a management approach, which focuses on the characteristics of the credit industry, its workings and the policies adopted by supply-side players; a legal approach, which investigates the impact the regulatory framework has on competition and consumer protection; a socio-psychological approach, which analyses how individuals are affected by consumption behaviour and indebtedness choices; an economic approach, which for the most part concentrates on the determinants of the demand for and supply of consumer credit and on an analysis of the characteristics of individuals and households in debt.

In this chapter we will discuss the economic approach with the aim of providing an outline of the individual and institutional factors that are considered in the literature as determinants of consumer credit, its diffusion and distribution amongst different segments of the population.

The economic models referred to are based on the economic rationality of individuals, who seek to increase living standards by smoothing consumption over different periods of their lives through saving and borrowing decisions. According to these models, consumer credit demand and supply is determined by individual factors, i.e. socio-demographic and economic factors, as well as by institutional factors, i.e. the institutional context in which borrowers and lenders are placed.

These studies, which first appeared in the second half of the twentieth century, have been flanked in recent years by work in behavioural economics, which focuses instead on the psychological variables that influence an individual's behaviour and which have revealed that this behaviour is at odds with the rational choices posited by traditional economic models.

The analysis of the literature offered here, rather than attempting to represent an exhaustive summary of empirical estimations and economic models used by the authors of the various works cited, more modestly aims to provide a basis for specific investigations into the diffusion of consumer credit in Europe, the nature of the consumer credit industry, the causes of over-indebtedness and the most appropriate policy responses to the problem.

1.2 The Life-Cycle and Permanent Income Theories

The theoretical economic framework for consumption, saving and indebtedness decisions is developed within the Life-Cycle theory, developed by Modigliani and Brumberg in 1954, and the Permanent Income Hypothesis, proposed by Friedman in 1957.[1]

The central idea of these intertemporal consumption choice models is that households make their consumption choices (and consequently those relating to saving and indebtedness) on the basis of their wealth, current disposable income and future income expectations so as to guarantee a uniform level of consumption over their lifetimes.

The underlying assumption of these models is that income is generally low in an individual's early working life and tends to rise towards retirement. Individuals at the start of their working life, expecting higher future income receipts, finance the purchase of assets in order to raise consumption over the level offered by current income. Nearing the end of their working lives, inversely, individuals raise savings levels in preparation for retirement when spending will be greater than earnings. Within this framework, saving and indebtedness guarantee heightened economic welfare by smoothing out consumption over time.

In the "standard theory", named as such by Modigliani himself, the economic model posits that choices regarding households' consumption levels over different periods of their life are subject to an intertemporal budget constraint. Consequently, they may decide in a certain year to spend more than available income by running down all or part of their assets and/or by borrowing, provided that such a solution is temporary and that they die solvent.[2]

Considerable further empirical analyses of the theory have stressed the need for the standard model to take into account two additional aspects (Ando and Modigliani 1957; Modigliani et al. 1985; Modigliani 1988; Deaton 1992; Alessie et al. 1997; Attanasio 1999):

– Households demand for debt is subject to factors other than income and wealth;
– households may be "liquidity constrained".

---

[1] Although the two theories use different economic models, both envisage similar consumption behaviour patterns. For the purposes of this work, therefore, the names of both will be considered as equivalents.
[2] For an analysis of the dynamic consumption theory, see Bagliano and Bertola (2004).

Table 1.1 Consumer credit demand and supply factors

	INDIVIDUAL FACTORS	
	Socio-demographic	
	Age	
	Education	
	Size and composition of family	
	...	
	Economic	
CREDIT DEMAND	Income	CREDIT SUPPLY
	Wealth	
	Uncertainty	
	...	
	INSTITUTIONAL FACTORS	
	Efficiency of justice system	
	Information-sharing	
	Informal credit markets	
	...	

Encompassing these aspects effectively implies the model should address variables that influence both the demand and supply sides of the credit market (Table 1.1).

These variables can be either "individual" or "institutional". Individual factors regard the characteristics of an individual and his/her household and can be classified into two classes: socio-demographic (for example, age, size and composition of the family, education) and economic (for example, employment status, work profiles, financial assets).

Institutional factors that characterise local credit markets include the justice system, the existence and quality of information-sharing mechanisms amongst financial institutions, and the presence of informal credit circuits (borrowing from relatives and friends).

The same variables, individual and institutional, influence both credit demand and supply, albeit not always to the same extent and in the same direction.[3]

1.2.1 Credit Demand Factors

With regards to individual factors, empirical analysis has extended the standard model by examining to what extent socio-demographic variables, such as the age of the head of the household, the size and make up of the family, and levels of education, influence individuals' spending, saving and borrowing choices.[4]

---

[3] See Sect. 1.5 for a summary of the variables influencing the demand for and supply of credit.

[4] The term "household" refers in the literature both to an individual and a family with personal loan commitments. For this reason when reference is made in this work to "household unsecured debt" the terms "individual" and "family" are considered as synonyms.

Consistent with the life-cycle, young people, characterised by expectations of rising income receipts, have a strong demand for credit which, over time, drops because income is sufficient to cover spending and with age individuals become more adverse to indebtedness.

Indebtedness is higher or the capacity to save is lower also in the case of large families with children at pre-school or school age when in this life-cycle phase spending is typically high. This being said, however, the presence of children may also be an incentive for greater saving in order to satisfy inter-generational asset transfer.

Education also has a positive effect on the demand for credit both because it reflects a probable rise in future income and greater job security and reduces the costs of entering the credit market thanks to an enhanced capacity to make informed decisions regarding indebtedness.

In addition to the economic variables already included in the original framework, i.e. individuals' income and wealth, empirical analysis has extended the model to include also uncertainty about the amount and variability of future income. Such uncertainty determines the need to retain liquidity as a precaution against income falls or unexpected increases in liabilities, with a subsequent increase in saving and a reduction in the demand for credit.

Economic models ascribe uncertainty principally to the type of employment and related employment contract. For this reason, recourse to debt on the part of individuals with greater uncertainty regarding their future income, such as young people or individuals with temporary employment contracts, is less than could be expected if such a variable were not included in the model.

Turning to institutional factors, the literature identifies three in particular: the extent of information-sharing amongst financial institutions regarding the level of borrowers' credit risk, the efficiency of the justice system in taking steps against insolvent individuals, and the size of the informal credit market.

Institutional factors influence the demand for credit by creating the conditions for the market to sanction opportunistic behaviour. The decision to repay a loan depends in fact not only on the capacity, but also on the willingness of an individual to respect the contractual obligations undersigned. Put another way, a household may decide to take out a loan not as a way of anticipating spending based on expectations of increased future income receipts, but because he/she knows that the loan will not be repaid; a phenomenon aptly termed as "strategic insolvency" (Gropp et al. 1997).

An evaluation of the costs and benefits of insolvency will influence an individual's decision whether to respect the contractual terms of the loan or whether to default. Such a decision will be influenced by the credit market's capacity to sanction effectively opportunistic behaviour.

Information-sharing mechanisms amongst lenders reduce a household's incentive to over-borrow by demanding credit to more than one institution at the same time as each lender will be in a position to know the applicant's total system-wide exposure.

With regards to the efficiency of the justice system, the probability of late payments or insolvency increases when credit recovery procedures are costly and lengthy.

Turning to the third institutional factor – the role of informal credit markets – individuals who have access to loans from relatives and friends will regard the possible exclusion from formal credit circuits as less problematical thanks to the fact that when in need they can always turn to informal credit solutions.

1.2.2 Credit Supply Factors

The standard model assumes that there are no constraints on the part of the household to obtain credit. The amount of the loan, however, is either subject to a ceiling or the level of interest rates applied by lenders may reduce or cancel the demand for credit, so forcing households to limit their spending to the resources available. In other words, many households will not be able to borrow according to their needs or to the extent posited by the variables so far discussed.

Credit constraints are widely viewed in the literature as deriving from the existence of asymmetric information between borrowers and lenders;[5] such informational imperfections force lenders to take steps to avoid approving loans that will subsequently not be repaid. In turn, credit availability by financial intermediaries depends on an individual's socio-demographic and economic characteristics as well as his/her institutional setting.

As to individual factors, high income and wealth levels combined with conditions of stable employment increase the supply of credit offered by lenders.

With regards to the impact of institutional factors on the supply side, two of the three factors previously mentioned in the analysis of the demand side are particularly significant: the efficiency of the justice system and the existence of information-sharing mechanisms.

An efficient justice system allows lenders to recover non-performing loans rapidly at contained costs. This is clearly the case with secured debt exposures: delays and difficulties in obtaining the repossession of mortgaged property act as disincentives for lenders to extend their mortgage loan portfolio.

The same institutional factor may also have an impact on the supply of unsecured credit: in this case, the disciplinary effect on insolvent individuals is represented by information concerning them and collected by credit bureaus that may damage their prospects of accessing the credit market again in the future. In such

---

[5]Asymmetric information, deriving from the fact that borrowers have more information regarding the probability of default in comparison to lenders, gives rise to problems of adverse selection and moral hazard. The first, which occurs during the evaluation of the borrower's financial position aimed at deciding whether to grant the loan and if so at what price, refers to situations in which those borrowers prepared to pay higher rates of interest presumably represent a higher level of risk as they know that the probability of repaying the loan is low. Moral hazard occurs after the loan has been granted; the higher the rate of interest, the greater the probability is that borrowers will embark on high risk projects and consequently lenders will apply a price beyond which the loan application will be rejected (Stiglitz and Weiss 1981; Frexias and Rochet 1997).

a scenario, the availability of credit is affected by the existence amongst lenders of information-sharing mechanisms which are used in building up customer credit-risk profiles and which therefore reduce asymmetric information.

In practical terms, banks try to overcome moral hazard and adverse selection problems by the screening and monitoring of customers' credit-risk profiles. In particular, with regards to personal loans, the total amount of which does not justify individual detailed credit-risk evaluations, lenders use credit scoring procedures that identify counterpart risk profiles and as a result reject or accept applications on the basis of insolvency projections generated by the model.[6]

1.3 Empirical Findings

Empirical analyses aimed at studying the determinants of household credit markets and their coherence with Life-Cycle and Permanent Income models focus on the following areas, according to the research questions they investigate:

- Participation in the credit market
- Level of borrowing
- Cross-country characteristics
- Risk of over-indebtedness
- Credit constraints

Work across these areas examines both individual and institutional variables. Analysis has typically concentrated on the demand side, though a branch of study has used economic models to investigate the determinants of the supply of consumer credit (Table 1.2).

1.3.1 Participation in the Credit Market

Empirical analyses in this area indicate the determinants of households' participation in the credit market.

Amongst socio-economic factors examined within the individual category, the age profile as a determinant of having unsecured debt is consistent with the life-cycle model of consumption: young people are more likely to borrow than members of older age groups (Crook 2006; Fabbri and Padula 2004), with the percentage of individuals with unsecured debt peaking for individuals aged between 30 and 40 years of age (Del Rio and Young 2005a; Magri 2007).

---

[6]For an overview of the literature of credit scoring and the personal characteristics associated with insolvency risk see Thomas et al. (2002) and a dedicated edition of the *Journal of Operational Research Society* (January 2001).

1.3 Empirical Findings

Table 1.2 The literature of household credit

Topic area	Authors	Year
Participation in the credit market	Gropp, Scholz, White	1997
	Magri	2002, 2007
	Fay, Hurst, White	2002
	Fabbri, Padula	2004
	Del Rio, Young	2005a
	Crook	2006
	Grant, Padula	2006, 2007
	Casolaro, Gambacorta, Guiso	2006
	Jappelli, Pagano	2006
	Duygan, Grant	2008
Level of borrowing	Magri	2002, 2007
	Fabbri, Padula	2004
	Del Rio, Young	2005a
Cross-country characteristics	Bianco, Jappelli, Pagano	2002
	Crook	2006
	Crook, Hochguertel	2007
Risk of over-indebtedness	Bridges, Disney	2004
	Del Rio, Young	2005b
	Rinaldi, Sanchez-Arellano	2006
Credit constraints	Cox, Jappelli	1993
	Ferri, Simon	2000
	Magri	2002, 2007
	Fabbri, Padula	2004
	Crook	2006
	Bicakova	2007

With regards to household size, Fabbri and Padula (2004) find that there is a positive relation between levels of indebtedness and the number of household members. Similarly, Del Rio and Young (2005) and Crook (2006) show that married individuals are more likely to have unsecured debt than the non-married.

Having higher educational qualifications is associated with a higher probability of having unsecured debt (Grant 2003; Del Rio and Young 2005a). This fact is supported by empirical results provided in the literature, which suggest a higher level of educational qualifications is a robust proxy of rising future earnings and greater information-processing skills, with the cost-savings this generates when participating in the credit market. The authors however suggest that this relationship exists for secured debt and is less significant for consumer credit, which is usually unsecured.

Levels of education in general can reasonably be seen to have a positive impact on individuals' financial knowledge: the higher this level of knowledge is, the easier it is to access and evaluate financial products and services. This aspect should logically play an important role where complex products or large loan amounts, such as mortgages, are concerned. In fact, educational qualifications appear to be a less important factor for simple, easy-to-understand small loan packages, which are distributed not only by lenders over-the-counter, but also directly by retail stores. Ferri and Simon (2000) use the ratio between cash and financial instruments as a proxy for individuals' educational levels and report that the lower the ratio, the higher the level of financial expertise which, in turn, raises awareness regarding the decision to borrow.

Fabbri and Padula (2004) and Magri (2002) analyse the effect of town and city size on indebtedness and report that residents in smaller towns have a lower probability of having debt. The authors propose the greater presence of informal credit circuits in these contexts as an explanation.

Turning to economic factors, the income variable is of significant importance. Demand for credit is positively influenced by expectations of increased future receipts, as posited by the life-cycle theory: if there were no expectations of increased income in the future, there would be no need to advance spending via debt (Ferri and Simon 2000; Crook 2005; Cox and Jappelli 1993).

As to current income levels, Fabbri and Padula (2004), consistent with many studies carried out in the United States, reveal a positive relation between levels of debt and current income. Del Rio and Young (2005a) and Magri (2007) show that for middle-range levels of income, the marginal utility of consumption is high and income rises can generate higher spending and subsequent increased demand for credit. Crook (2006) also shows that high-income individuals have a greater probability of having debt also due to the probability of facing fewer supply side constraints. The effect of the income variable however becomes less marked for middle-to-high earners, who, as their incomes rise, are able to satisfy spending needs from income.

Findings differ with regards to low income as a factor for indebtedness: Del Rio and Young (2005a) show that there is less probability of the poorer paid having debt due to the fact that low earnings are typically associated with highly unstable employment conditions that tend to reduce both the demand for and the supply of credit. Cox and Jappelli (1993), on the other hand, find a negative relationship between low income and probability of having debt as individuals currently at the bottom of the salary scale have expectations of increased earnings in the future and consequently borrow to smooth consumption over their life times.

Net wealth is also an important factor.[7] The percentage of households that have debt is higher for those with limited net wealth. In fact, results in the literature show that households with high net wealth are able to satisfy their consumption needs autonomously without recourse to debt. In particular, Magri (2002) shows that rises in wealth are tracked by falls in the demand for consumer credit as spending can be financed autonomously. However, households with intermediate wealth levels are more likely to participate in the consumer credit market due to increased spending patterns that characterise improvements in life style. Del Rio and Young (2005a) focus their analysis on households with a portfolio of financial assets and find that

---

[7]Net wealth being an individual's total financial and real assets after deducting financial liabilities.

1.3 Empirical Findings

households that do not own such a portfolio have a greater probability of having unsecured debt than those who do.

As regards labour market status, consistent with the theoretical models that consider uncertainty about future income as a factor that reduces borrowing, empirical evidence shows that demand for personal loans is higher amongst the employed in comparison to the self-employed, who are subject to greater uncertainty regarding future income (Crook 2006; Magri 2007). The retired have a lower probability of having debt as a result of the age effect, i.e. no further expectations of rising future income. The unemployed also are less likely to participate in the credit market (Del Rio and Young 2005a). This latter finding, which contrasts with the Permanent Income theory's postulate that those temporarily without a job should increase their demand for credit, is based on two constraints: firstly, the unemployed individual's pessimism regarding his/her future work prospects and, secondly, supply-side restrictions.

Moving to institutional factors, analysis has focused on the probability of lenders' having their loans repaid.

Studies show how the probability of default is negatively correlated with the level of efficiency of the justice system and the existence of effective information-sharing mechanisms, whilst positively correlated with the existence of informal credit markets.

Specifically with regards to the efficiency of the justice system, Duygan and Grant (2008) show that the probability of late payment or insolvency increases as legal costs and repossession or foreclosure times rise; both facts act as incentives for opportunistic behaviour on the part of borrowers. The authors also find that a sudden fall in income, due to, for instance, job loss, will more probably lead to default in legal systems where creditor protection is weak. Grant and Padula (2006) however underline that the effect of this institutional factor is limited to mortgages and has little impact on unsecured debt forms, such as consumer credit. Gropp et al. (1997) and Fay et al. (2002) refer specifically to "strategic default" and, with regards to the United States, find that the probability of insolvency is higher when disciplinary mechanisms are ineffective, such as bankruptcy laws which favour the insolvent individual by fixing relatively high levels of income and wealth outside the threshold fixed in bankruptcy proceedings, and when the individual's social context is marked by high levels of insolvency and therefore where there is less stigma relating to the phenomenon.

Japelli and Pagano (2006) show how the existence of information-sharing mechanisms reduces an individual's incentive to over-borrow by applying for credit at more than one institution at the same time as each lender is in a position to know the individual's total debt exposure to the system. Duygan and Grant (2006) also show that the likelihood of insolvency is less when the financial system is equipped to know about previous episodes of insolvency and whether such events are due to adverse events, such as job loss.

As regards the role of informal credit markets, Grant and Padula (2006) highlight that it has a significant economic and statistical effect on debt repayment and negatively impacts attitudes to repayment: individuals that have access to loans from family members or friends consider the possible exclusion from the credit market as less costly because, if in need, they can always turn to informal credit solutions. Access to informal credit therefore increases the probability of insolvency on formal markets as such availability encourages opportunistic behaviour.

1.3.2 Level of Borrowing

As far as this second research area, i.e. the amount of debt held by households, among individual factors age does not appear to influence the level of borrowing, whilst the level of educational qualifications is positively correlated (Magri 2007; Del Rio and Young 2005a).

As regards economic variables, Fabbri and Padula (2004) show that income and wealth levels have a positive effect on the amount of unsecured debt an individual is likely to have.

With reference to labour market status, Magri (2007) finds that the amount of consumer credit is higher for the self-employed and suggests this is because individuals in this category use unsecured debt also as a means of funding their work activities.

The impact of institutional variables does not differ from those illustrated in the first topic area (Sect. 1.3.1): the existence of inefficient systems of justice, ineffective information-sharing mechanisms and extensive informal credit markets not only increases the probability of participation in the credit market, but also the amount of debt held by households.

1.3.3 Cross-Country Analyses

The third research area consists of spatial analyses of the determinants of unsecured debt with the aim of investigating the existence of any factors that are specific to a country or geographical area.

Results of work carried out in this field, though based on heterogeneous databases, highlight, apart from significant differences in terms of the percentage of individuals' having debt and the level of debt expressed as a share of GDP and individual income, important differences regarding individual determinants of demand for consumer credit.

Crook (2006) points out that as regards age, although the probability of having debt in all countries is greater for young people, the maximum percentage is reached in the United Kingdom and Germany (those aged 30–40) and later (those aged 40–50) in the United States, Japan and the Netherlands.

The percentage of households having unsecured debt is positively correlated with income. Evidence supporting this position is particularly strong in the United

Kingdom and the United States, where the share of middle-to-high income earners with debt is very high, whilst only at marginal levels in Italy.

With reference to employment status, though the retired have a generally low probability of having debt, the share of those with debt is higher in the United Kingdom and Germany. There is less probability of the self-employed having debt in Italy and the Netherlands, whereas the unemployed have greater problems in accessing credit in Spain and the United States (Crook and Hochguertel 2007).

Cross-country analyses reveal the effect of institutional factors. Studies show that though the set of individual variables influencing demand for credit are common across countries, significant differences emerge regarding how individuals respond to negative shocks: the same event, for instance job loss, is met by default in certain institutional environments, typically those characterised by inefficient justice systems, and repayment in others. Such differences cannot be explained solely on the basis of individuals' deviant behaviour with regard to debt, but also on the basis of differences in the efficiency and effectiveness of institutional factors (Bianco et al. 2002; Crook 2006).

1.3.4 Over-Indebtedness

This field of research attempts to identify institutional factors that may determine situations of financial fragility or over-indebtedness which increase the probability that individuals will not be able to repay their debts.

Such situations of financial tension or difficulty are described in the literature as adverse events that can transform a performing loan into one the borrower finds difficult to repay. Such negative shocks to household finances include job loss, illness or divorce.

The most significant statistical variable for identifying critical repayment difficulties is the level of debt to income. Del Rio and Young (2005b) show that there is a positive relation between the level of debt to income and the probability of repayment difficulties.

Similarly, Rinaldi and Sanchez-Arellano (2006) report that a rise in the debt/income ratio is associated with an increase in payment arrears. The same authors however also point out that if a rise in the debt/income ratio is accompanied by an increase in available income, the negative effects of increased indebtedness are cancelled out. Bridges and Disney (2004) identify low incomes as the main cause for over-indebtedness and insolvency.

The models referred to generally include dummy variables in order to capture unexpected events that may have a negative economic impact. The effects such events can have on a borrower's financial position vary noticeably from country to country and depend on institutional factors which, as already seen, can influence a household's willingness to repay a loan.

1.3.5 Credit Constraints

The last research area analyses the existence of credit constraints as a means of identifying both the socio-economic profile of individuals most at risk of having their application for a loan turned down and the effect institutional factors have on lenders' credit supply.

As regards individual factors, empirical evidence concurs that the supply of credit rises with increases in age and educational qualifications; it also tends to rise for married couples and large families (Crook 2006; Cox and Jappelli 1993).

The size of the town or city of residence, which is a significant determinant of demand for credit, does not have a significant impact on the supply side (Magri 2007).

With reference to economic variables, as one may expect, the probability of having a loan application rejected is negatively correlated with income and wealth levels. Loan applications from the self-employed have a greater probability of rejection than those presented by the employed (Fabbri and Padula 2004; Ferri and Simon 2000).

Empirical analyses into the effect institutional variables have on the credit supply side concentrate principally on the specific features of the justice system and the existence of information-sharing mechanisms in a particular country or geographic area.

Casolaro et al. (2006) analyse the availability of credit in Italy and show that supply is influenced by a set of formal and informal mechanisms that determines repayment. As regards formal mechanisms, in line with Fabbri and Padula's findings (Fabbri and Padula 2004), Magri (2007) and Bianco et al. (2002) report that the more efficient a justice system is (efficiency here being measured in terms of the years necessary to close proceedings), the lower the costs for credit recovery are and subsequently the lower the probability of credit rationing. Fabbri and Padula (2004) state that when the justice system is efficient, not only is more credit available, but ceteris paribus the cost of credit is lower as is the amount of guarantees required. Magri (2002) highlights, however, how the efficiency of the justice system has less impact in the area of consumer credit.

The availability of credit also depends on the existence of informal credit mechanisms, normally determined on the basis of a community or geographical area's social capital. This resource is measured generally by the number of blood donations per capita, the level of trust individuals have in fellow community members, and participation in political elections (Guiso et al. 2004). It is proposed that higher levels of social capital correspond to a civic sense and a network of social relations that drive people to respect their individual commitments. Jappelli and Pagano (2006) show that, consistent with the literature, the effect of an efficient system of information-sharing about credit availability is positive.

Bicakova (2007) analyses the existence of asymmetric information (moral hazard and adverse selection) and its effects on the consumer credit market. She starts by showing that default rates differ according to the product for which the loan is taken out (loans for the purchase of motorbikes, second-hand cars, mobile phones have higher insolvency rates over those for new cars and electrical appliances) and she analyses whether this is due to the "selection effect" or the "good effect".

According to the first mechanism, individuals with high levels of insolvency risk will be more likely to purchase certain types of goods, such a motorbikes. The good effect, on the other hand, explains the existence of differing insolvency rates due to the fact that each good has specific features, such as short useful life or early obsolescence, which act as negative incentives to repay. On the basis of results which show the presence of both effects, the author believes that the unsecured debt market is affected by both adverse selection induced by the selection effect and moral hazard induced by the good effect, with both effects conditioning the availability of credit.

1.4 Behavioural Economics

Behavioural economics has in recent years proposed alternative theories to Life-Cycle and Permanent Income models (Brown et al. 2005; Karlsson et al. 2004; Ranyard et al. 2006; Stone and Vasquez Maury 2006; Supriya et al. 2005; Poppe 2008; Yang et al. 2007; Graham and Isaac 2002). These studies have focused on behavioural aspects that may significantly influence individuals' decisions relating to spending, saving or indebtedness. These aspects differ from the socio-demographic and economic variables analysed within the economic models discussed in the previous paragraphs.

The research models adopted within behavioural economics are based on empirical results and anomalies regarding consumer behaviour that conflict with traditional notions of economic rationality. Several studies have in fact shown how the behaviour of individuals deviates systematically from the "rational choice" model of standard economic theories without implying that such behaviour is irrational.[8]

Individual choices are influenced by psychological factors, such as personal taste, forecasting errors and impatience, which as a result prevent individuals from maximising future utility (Kilborn 2005; Meier and Sprenger 2007).

Three main psychological factors are identified in the literature as inducing individuals to make non rational borrowing choices:

− Overconfidence bias
− Availability heuristic
− Hyperbolic discounting

As regards the first, individuals tend to be over-optimistic about their own exposure to risk and believe that they are capable of managing their level of indebtedness. As a result, they systematically underestimate the probability of being hit by adverse events (illness, job loss, etc.) that can lead to financial fragility and over-indebtedness and over-estimate their capacities in managing household resources.

---

[8]Rationality as a concept adopted in economic theory consists in a series of hypothetical, regularised preferences on the part of an individual described by their utility function.

The availability heuristic means that individuals tend to estimate the probability of an event on the basis of the availability of the experience. In other words, individuals typically evaluate the likelihood of a negative event's occurring on the basis of the ease with which they can remember a similar previous event in their lifetime rather than on any objective analysis of probability.

The availability of the experience is influenced by how often, how important and how recent the event was. The more frequent and recent the event occurred, the more likely it is that individuals will overestimate the probability of a similar event happening again; vice versa, the less frequent and more remote in time the event took place, the more likely it is that individuals will underestimate the probability of a similar event's reoccurring. Consequently, if experiences of certain adverse events, such as liquidity crises, financial difficulties or over-indebtedness, are not available, individuals will tend to underestimate the chances of being affected by such events.

What is more, even if the same individuals were regularly exposed to statistics illustrating insolvency rates amongst other people, the impersonal nature of such information may mean it is not effective. Taking into account both excess optimism and the availability heuristic, it is clear that the probability of individuals' underestimating their exposure to insolvency risk is high.

The so-called hyperbolic discounting factor indicates how individuals tend to systematically overvalue immediate costs and benefits and undervalue those in the future. In other words, they give greater importance to present events in comparison to those in the future.

As regards the decision to participate in the credit market, the hyperbolic discount factor pushes individuals in the moment when they have to decide whether to purchase on credit terms or not to opt for immediate purchase. This decision is made despite the fact that an individual is rationally able to judge that the level of debt taken on is unsustainable in comparison to future income receipts.

The hyperbolic discount explains why individuals choose "buy now, pay later" solutions that bring immediate gratification at a future cost. Other forms of credit, such as revolving credit solutions, encourage forms of behaviour that respond to this psychological characteristic. The hyperbolic discount factor, in fact, means that individuals adopt impatient, short-sighted behaviour patterns which make it difficult for them to be fully aware of the consequences of their spending decisions on the sustainability of personal debt (Meier and Sprenger 2007).

The impact of the hyperbolic discount factor on consumer choices is heightened by the features of the social context in which an individual lives. Individuals, in fact, consume not only to satisfy basic needs, but also to have access to the power and prestige ownership of certain goods represents and to compensate for individual personality problems such as low self-esteem. Owning particular goods is therefore a conduit for satisfaction and success within a particular social reference group.

This social comparison becomes a crucial factor in the consumption decision as personal levels of satisfaction are evaluated in relation to the status of other individuals. As societies become increasingly more materialistic and consumerist, such competition clearly increases individuals' spending and their tendency to fund consumption by borrowing (Karlsson et al. 2004). The need to spend may in fact raise demand for credit without an individual's having a clear idea about what this involves. If the individual has a level of income below that of his/her social reference group, then the probability of over-spending and ending up in debt increases (Watson 2003).

Studies carried out within behavioural economics have also shown that individuals have little awareness of the existence and consequences these psychological mechanisms have. Indeed, individuals in financial difficulties tend to lay the blame on exogenous factors such as illness, divorce or job loss, which reduce incomes levels below those expected. Rarely do individuals recognise that the causes for their difficulties lie principally or at least also with their inability to manage money and the decisions made regarding spending and indebtedness. Furthermore, many studies have shown how deviant behaviour patterns persist even when individuals are aware of the risks they face. Individuals' incapacity to take corrective steps despite knowing of the dangers of over-indebtedness may have significant repercussions in designing effective policies for the management of situations of indebtedness that are already or are at risk of becoming pathological[9] (Kilborn 2005; Watson 2003; Lea et al. 1995).

1.5 Summary of the Determinants of the Demand for and Supply of Consumer Credit

The economic models of the Permanent Income and Life-Cycle theories continue to be used as a framework for analysis of households' consumption, saving and indebtedness decisions (Jappelli 2005).

However, work in behavioural economics has made an important contribution in drawing attention to the role played not only by socio-demographic and economic variables, but also psychological factors as determinants of the demand for unsecured debt. It has also been shown how psychological factors have an impact on the effectiveness of policies adopted to prevent ex ante and manage ex post financial difficulties arising from over-indebtedness.

Table 1.3 provides a summary of the factors influencing the demand for and supply of consumer credit. As can be seen, the signs (+) and (−) are not always homogeneous and have varying degrees of intensity.[10]

---

[9]For an analysis of the reasons for over-indebtedness see Chap. 4 and Sect. 4.2.2 in particular.

[10]This emerges clearly as regards institutional variables: if, on one hand, the existence of inefficient justice systems increases the demand for credit because this raises the number of strategic insolvencies, on the other, due to lengthy and costly credit recovery times, lenders reduce the levels of credit they are prepared to make available. As regards also psychological factors, the variables examined should have the opposite effect on the demand for credit in respect of the influence they exert on the supply side. However, in this case, i.e. information relating to personal inclinations, the problems for lenders generated by asymmetric information are particularly acute.

Table 1.3 Summary of the determinants of consumer credit

Possible relation with credit demand		Possible relation with credit supply
	INDIVIDUAL FACTORS	
	Socio-demographic	
(+) For young households with future income expectations (+) For adults	Age	(+) Less evident bell-curve
(+) Greater need for consumption	Size and composition of family	(+) For large families
(+) Higher levels of financial knowledge and better understanding of financial products	Level of educational qualifications	(+) Higher levels of financial knowledge and more responsible borrowing
(+) Reduced role of informal credit markets and greater availability of lenders	Size of town/city of residence	Not significant
	Economic	
(+) For middle-high income brackets	Income	(+) Higher probability of repayment
(+) For intermediate wealth levels	Wealth	(+) Higher probability of repayment
(−) Due to the need to hold savings in case of unexpected events	Uncertain future income	(−) Less probability of repayment
	Psychological	
(+) Over-estimate money management ability	Overconfidence bias	(−) Factor difficult to identify
(+) Under-estimate risk of over-indebtedness	Availability heuristic	(−) Factor difficult to identify
(+) Under-estimate of future sustainability of personal debt	Hyperbolic discount	(−) Factor difficult to identify
	INSTITUTIONAL FACTORS	
(−) Incentive for strategic insolvency	Efficiency of justice system	(+) Reduced recovery times and costs
(−) Incentive for strategic insolvency	Information-sharing systems	(+) Reduced information asymmetries
(+) Incentive for strategic insolvency	Informal credit market	(−) Incentive for strategic insolvency

These factors will be discussed in the chapters that follow and, in particular, during an analysis of the diffusion of consumer credit in Europe, the characteristics of individuals in debt, the most appropriate policies for the prevention and management of over-indebtedness and the lending policies adopted by the credit industry.

Chapter 2
Household Consumer Credit Demand

2.1 Introduction

Since the mid 1980s consumer credit has grown rapidly in most European countries. However, the amounts borrowed by households as a proportion of income differ widely from country to country. These differences can be ascribed to a variety of factors, some of which have been extensively analysed in the literature,[1] that influence the demand for and supply of credit and, consequently, the size of national household credit markets.

In this chapter we will examine, through the use of macroeconomic data, the evolution of national consumer credit markets. We will then analyse the social, demographic and economic characteristics of indebted households based on information available from national surveys carried out periodically by National Central Banks and/or statistics institutes.

2.2 Consumer Credit in Europe

Recent estimates indicate that overall outstanding amounts of consumer credit in Europe borrowed had reached around € 1,081 billion at year-end 2006 (Fig. 2.1).[2] Data relating to consumer credit volumes in absolute terms and not to more accurate parameters indicate in which countries this form of unsecured debt is most present. Almost 96% of the total refers, in fact, to EU-15, with three quarters of amounts owed concentrated in three markets: the United Kingdom (29.3%), Germany

---

[1] A detailed analysis of theoretical and empirical studies into the determinants of the demand for and supply of consumer credit is given in Chap. 1.

[2] The macroeconomic analysis was carried out using the 27 countries that currently make up the European Union. Any absence in charts 2.1–2.6 of one or more countries is due to unavailable data. In particular, consumer credit data are not available for Cyprus, which as a result is not included in the analysis.

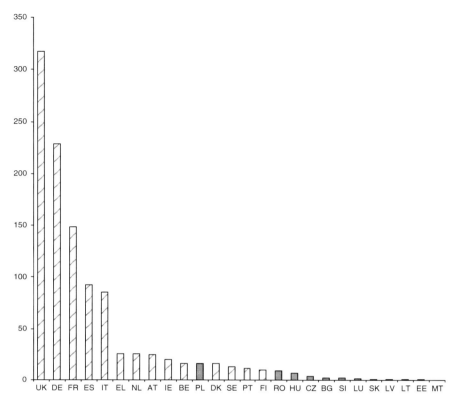

Fig. 2.1 Outstanding consumer credit in EU-27 countries (billions of euros)
Source: computations on national statistics (National Central Banks and Eurostat). Glossary of symbols: Austria (AT), Belgium (BE), Bulgaria (BL), Cyprus (CY), Czech Republic (CZ), Denmark (DK), Estonia (EE), Finland (FI), France (FR), Germany (DE), Greece (EL), Hungary (HU), Ireland (IE), Italy (IT), Latvia (LV), Lithuania (LT), Luxembourg (LU), Malta (MT), Netherlands (NL), Poland (PL), Portugal (PT), Romania (RO), Slovakia (SK), Slovenia (SI), Spain (ES), Sweden (SE), United Kingdom (UK). EU-15 countries are shown in *oblique lines*, whilst the new entrants are shown in *plain*

(21.1%) and France (13.8%). These are followed by Spain (8.5%) and Italy (7.9%), with the remaining countries of the group some way behind. New EU Member States have generally low levels of consumer credit, with Poland accounting for more than one third of the volumes of these countries.

2.2.1 The Diffusion of Consumer Credit

Further analysis of the diffusion and distribution of consumer credit through the use of various indicators reveals considerable differences between countries, even though the trend in the period 2000–2006 was of generalised growth.[3]

---

[3]The period under analysis could not be extended beyond 2000 due to a lack of data for many of the new EU Member States.

2.2 Consumer Credit in Europe

Figure 2.2 shows the consumer credit-GDP ratio for each country. The United Kingdom has the highest indicator with total consumer credit debt accounting for 16.3% of GDP; at the other extreme, the consumer credit-GDP ratio for Slovakia is 2.1%, 14 percentage points behind the UK.

The other four countries, in addition to the United Kingdom, in which almost all the outstanding consumer credit is concentrated – Germany, France, Spain and Italy (Fig. 2.1) – recorded the following consumer credit-GDP ratios: Germany 9.8%; Spain 9.5%; France 8.2%; Italy 6.6%.

The first three countries are all above the average EU-15 figure of 8.1%, but in terms of market importance come in, respectively, at third, sixth and eight positions. Italy is the only country of this group with a figure significantly below the EU-15 average.

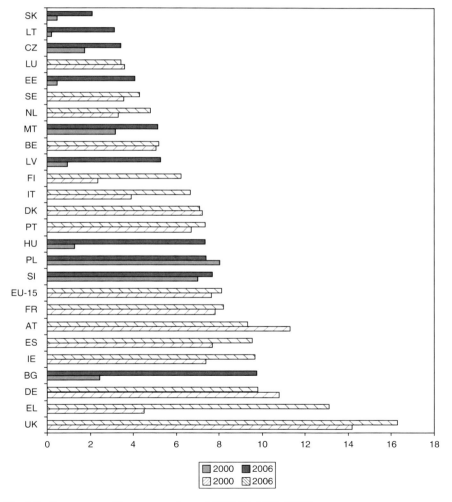

Fig. 2.2 Consumer credit as a percentage of GDP (%, 2000–2006)
Source: Computations on national statistics (National Central Banks and Eurostat)

Between 2000 and 2006, the level of household indebtedness in Spain overtook that recorded in France, principally on the back of macroeconomic factors, such as rising incomes, reduced unemployment, economic stability and cheaper borrowing interest rates (Bank of Spain 2004).

In France, conversely, growth in unsecured debt slowed; among other determinants, this was probably also a result of interest-rate ceilings fixed in national usury legislation[4] that are too low in relation to the profile of customers most at risk, i.e. low income earners and individuals in irregular employment, and which may have led to a reduction in the supply of credit (Davydoff and Naacke 2005).

Bulgaria, with a consumer credit-GDP ratio of 9.8%, is the only new entrant to record a figure higher than the EU-15 average. This can be put down, on the demand side, to strong economic growth and rising salaries and, on the supply side, high interest margins on retail lending that make this segment particularly attractive (Bulgarian National Bank 2007). Another significant characteristic of the Bulgarian situation is that a part of unsecured borrowing by households is used to funding small enterprises rather than financing domestic spending. In Bulgaria, in fact, small and medium-sized enterprises, which make up 99% of all businesses, run up against considerable difficulties in accessing credit, especially in the first years of activity when they are not able to provide the "hard information" (financial statements and reports) banks need to grant loans. As a result, small enterprises, which can provide only "soft information", such as family details, projects and ideas, use informal credit circuits made up by family and friends, who are able to borrow, mainly in the form of personal loans, more easily[5] (Tardieu 2007).

A comparison between the years 2000 and 2006 reveals two important trends: the first, as has already been noted, is that consumer credit in Europe recorded constant growth, with levels in some countries, such as in Greece and Bulgaria, reaching in only a few years EU-15 average levels after starting from comparatively immature credit market conditions; the second is that in some countries, such as the United Kingdom, France and Spain, where amounts borrowed in the form of consumer credit already represented a high percentage of GDP in 2000, growth rates, albeit down, continued to be positive, so demonstrating the increasing importance of this form of unsecured debt in these economies.

The role of consumer credit in European economies can be analysed also on the basis of the consumer credit to disposable income and consumer credit to consumption expenditure ratios. The first is most frequently used in the analysis of households' levels of indebtedness as well as in cross-country studies,[6] whilst the second measures the share of debt-financed spending.

---

[4] Article 313–3, *Code de la Consommation*.

[5] "Family policy is likely to have an impact on firm creation: subsidies to large families, easier access to credit for housing or lower taxes are elements that may have unexpected effects on business creation through the channel of informal loans. An easier access to credit for housing may lead business creators to ask for that type of credit in order to have access to a financial basis that could also be used to start a business" (Tardieu 2007).

[6] For an example of cross-country analyses, see European Central Bank (2006).

2.2 Consumer Credit in Europe

On the basis of the consumer credit to disposable income ratio (Fig. 2.3), broad differences can be found between European countries which run from a maximum of 25.5% in the United Kingdom to a minimum of 3.6% in Slovakia. In Ireland (19.9%), Denmark (15.6%), Germany (15.1%), Spain (14.9%), Austria (14.5%) and Greece (14.4%) the consumer credit to disposable income ratio is above the UE-15 average, whilst the figure for France is almost in line. In Belgium (8.9%) and Sweden (8.8%) the level of indebtedness is relatively low. Italy (8.4%) is also in this group, but recorded a marked increase over the 4.5% figure recorded in 2000 as a result also of progressive falls in the level of savings which increased the demand for debt (Bank of Italy 2006).

As regards the consumer credit to household consumer expenditure ratio, Fig. 2.4 illustrates distribution patterns similar to those seen for the consumer credit to disposable income ratio. The United Kingdom has the highest level of debt

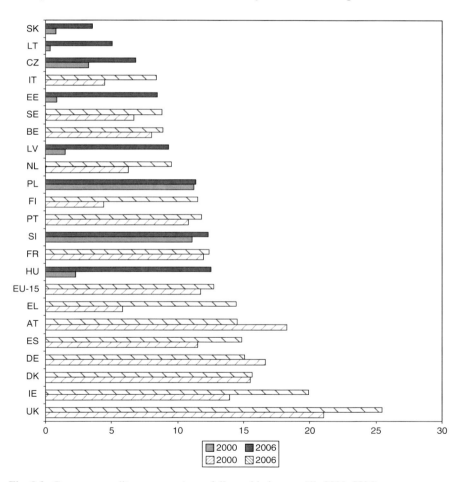

Fig. 2.3 Consumer credit as a percentage of disposable income (%, 2000–2006)
Source: Computations on national statistics (National Central Banks and Eurostat)

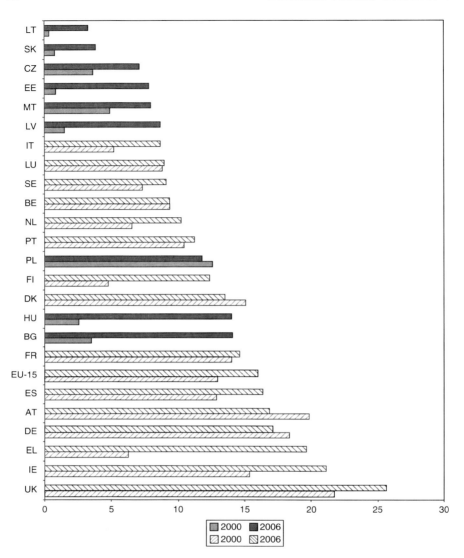

Fig. 2.4 Consumer credit as a percentage of consumption expenditure (%, 2000–2006)
Source: Computations on national statistics (National Central Banks and Eurostat)

financed spending (25.6%), followed by Ireland (21.1%) and Greece (19.6%). The rapid expansion of unsecured debt in Greece, which in only a few years has pushed diffusion of the country's consumer credit market beyond the EU-15 average, came on the back of strong economic growth and a generalised deregulation and liberalisation of the financial system (International Monetary Fund 2006).

Ratios recorded in the new Member States are on the whole contained, despite being markedly up on 2000. Amongst the EU-15 countries, Italy has the lowest figure: for every 100 euros of private spending, only 8.7% is financed by consumer credit.

2.2.2 Consumer Credit Growth Rates

Average growth rates for consumer credit between 2000 and 2006 (Fig. 2.5) suggest that differences between European countries shown so far are destined to narrow in the near future: growth rates in unsecured debt in less mature markets are high, also due to low initial levels, and continue to move closer to the European average (European Central Bank 2006).

Consumer credit growth rates are positive throughout Europe, especially in countries that recently joined the Union, where the diffusion of consumer credit is still limited: Lithuania (424%), Estonia (285%), Latvia (165%), Hungary (156%) and Slovakia (119%).

Amongst EU-15 countries, Greece has the highest rate of growth (60.6%), which has led the country in recent years to join those countries with the highest consumer credit to disposable income and consumer credit to household spending ratios. In Italy and the Netherlands, too, growth rates over the last few years have been

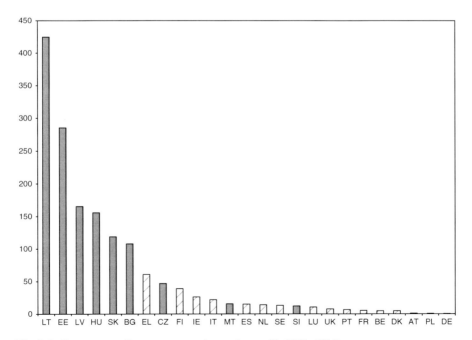

Fig. 2.5 Consumer credit average annual growth rate (%, 2000–2006)
Source: Computations on national statistics (National Central Banks and Eurostat)

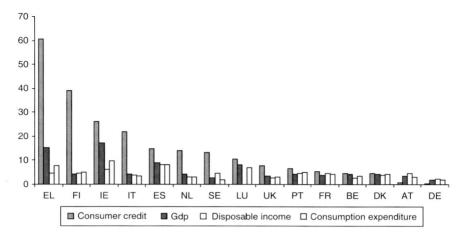

Fig. 2.6 Comparison of growth rates in EU-15 countries (%, 2000–2006)
Source: Computations on national statistics (National Central Banks and Eurostat)

significant. Germany and Austria recorded the lowest rates of growth along with a fall in the total amount of debt outstanding.

It is worth pointing out that, though consumer credit growth rates in some countries are undoubtedly the result of starting from scratch, it is however significant that growth is everywhere at levels higher than those recorded by disposable income and is accompanied by an increased tendency to spend rather than save.

This tendency is certainly evident in new entrant countries, which have three-figure growth rates, but also in EU-15 countries characterised by mature financial markets and developed economic systems (Fig. 2.6).

2.2.3 Heterogeneous Markets: Possible Causes

The considerable differences recorded amongst European markets, measured on the basis of a variety of indicators, can be put down to several factors, many of which idiosyncratic, which together interact and determine the degree of consumer credit penetration in a local economy.

In the forefront are structural factors, such as the institutional setting and contextual features that distinguish one national economy from another. Individuals' savings and spending decisions, which at the end of the day condition the diffusion of unsecured borrowing, are influenced both by macroeconomic variables, such as disposable income, consumption expenditure, interest rates, trends which vary from country to country, and welfare policies adopted by each country which, within the European Union differ considerably in terms of the existence and coverage of pension systems, public healthcare and education (European Central Bank 2006).

2.2 Consumer Credit in Europe

Another important factor that differentiates economies is the efficiency of a country's justice system which, as we have seen in the overview of the literature provided in Chap 1,[7] influences both the demand for and, above all, the supply of consumer credit given that where credit recovery times are lengthy and costs high, the financial system has fewer incentives to expand its lending activities.

In addition, the presence of large scale retailers in an economic system impacts significantly the diffusion of personal loans for the purchase of goods (Banque Nationale de Belgique 2004).

Each country is also characterised by the differing sizes of informal or parallel credit circuits, which typically flourish in immature financial markets.[8]

The extent of recourse to unsecured debt depends also on socio-cultural factors, such as individuals' savings habits and attitudes – positive or negative – to indebtedness. Thrift and/or an aversion to debt are, in fact, in some European countries historically more pronounced than in others with similar levels of economic development.

The reasons why an individual decides to participate in the credit market also influence the diffusion of unsecured borrowing in an economy: it is likely that, above all in emerging economies, consumer credit is used not only to finance spending, but also to support small businesses (Tardieu 2007).

A further factor that plays a part in affecting the spread of consumer credit amongst households is the nature of the credit industry itself. Deregulation and liberalisation, which have had an impact on all financial markets (albeit with differing timescales and to varying degrees), as well as technological innovations for the measurement and management of credit risk, have raised competition levels amongst financial intermediaries which, in turn, has led to increased credit availability at lower costs.

Nevertheless, significant differences still exist between countries regarding the characteristics of lenders and their aggressiveness in offering consumer credit solutions. On this point, the capability, for instance, of offering innovative products or of using innovation as a means of improving credit scoring methods as well as business size, which lenders depend on in order to extract economies of scale, will have significant effects on reducing the administration and management charges typically incurred in the supply of large quantities of comparatively small loans.

In new markets, such as those of the new Member States, the size of a credit market will be considerably affected by banks' strategic choices, for instance, the presence of banks that decide to focus on consumer credit rather than lending to enterprises because this range of products is considered less risky, easier to analyse thanks to standardised scoring procedures and more in line with a policy of expansion on the retail side.

---

[7]See in particular Gropp et al. (1997), Duygan and Grant (2008), Fay et al. (2002), Grant and Padula (2006).

[8]For an analysis of how the existence of information sharing mechanisms amongst lenders affects credit availability, see Jappelli and Pagano (2006).

The analysis so far has shown not only the raft of macroeconomic and idiosyncratic factors that explain the existence of heterogeneous credit markets in Europe, but above all the tendency throughout the area of growth across these markets. If, on one hand, there is little doubt that increased availability of consumer credit has improved households' economic conditions by smoothing consumption over time,[9] there are however raising concerns that the increasing use of consumer credit may cause serious difficulties amongst households that are financially fragile and exposed to the risk of over-indebtedness. These difficulties will have evident repercussions not only for the individuals and households affected, but also for the stability of the economic and financial system as a whole.

At this stage, therefore, any investigation into the growth of unsecured borrowing by households should necessarily address the socio-demographic and economic characteristics of those holding consumer credit.

2.3 Characteristics of Indebted Households

The aim of the following analysis of the socio-demographic (sex, age, educational qualifications, etc.) and economic (income, financial wealth) characteristics of individuals as determinants of participation in the unsecured debt market is to identify which segments of the population are more likely to use, or make greater use of, consumer credit and why, also in the light of evidence emerging from a review of the literature.[10]

In fact, on one hand, according to theory, individuals borrow to smooth out consumption over time and improve their living standards, whilst on the other, explanations outside the standard life-cycle model suggest that individuals may borrow not to maximise intertemporal utility, but to manage conditions of financial difficulty.

In the following paragraphs, we will, in addition to providing an outline of the characteristics of individuals that use consumer credit, compare debt behaviour of households in three different economic and institutional contexts and then highlight, where this is possible on the basis of data available, any temporal patterns, focusing on whether and how borrowers' characteristics change over time.

The analysis concentrates on three countries, Italy, Spain and the United Kingdom, where authoritative national surveys are carried out that provide datasets for further research. The diffusion of consumer credit in the three countries in question varies, a fact that makes the present enquiry all the more interesting.

---

[9] See Chap 1 for a review of economic models within Permanent Income and Life-Cycle theories that analyse spending, savings and indebtedness choices.

[10] See Chap 1 Sect. 1.2.

2.3.1 The Purpose of the Analysis

This section examines evidence from the following three surveys of household finances: Italy – *Indagine sui Bilanci delle Famiglie* (Survey of Household Income and Wealth, SHIW); Spain – *Encuesta Financiera de las Familias* (Survey of Household Finances – EFF); United Kingdom – British Household Panel Survey (BHPS).

These surveys provide information relating to socio-demographic characteristics, income, net wealth and indebtedness from representative samples of households.

Table 2.1 summarises the characteristics and methodologies of the three surveys.

The time frame used in this analysis as regards Italy is the period 2000–2006 during which four surveys were carried out.

For Spain, this empirical investigation relates to 2002 and 2005, the only two surveys available at the moment.

For what concerns the United Kingdom, the analysis uses the latest available survey (2005) and compares it with findings from the 2000 survey (wave 10). Waves 11 (2001), 12 (2002), 13 (2003) and 14 (2004) are not used as these do not include data referring to household indebtedness, which is monitored on a five-year basis.

The heterogeneousness of the databases, in terms of the content and form of the questionnaires as well as their frequency, does not weaken the validity of our findings due to the fact that all three surveys contain information relating to household indebtedness as well as to variables that provide a picture of the socio-demographic and economic profiles of individuals holding consumer credit.

We have established in three stages the variables for the analysis of borrowers present in each of the three surveys[11]:

Table 2.1 Principal features of the three surveys

	SHIW	EFF	BHPS
Institution responsible	Bank of Italy	Bank of Spain	UK Data Archive[a]
Frequency of interviews	Every 2 years[b]	Every 3 years	Every year
First year of survey	1987	2002	1991
Number of sampled households (last survey)	7,768	5,962	10,000
Number of household panels (last survey)	3,957	2,580	10,000[c]
Basis of survey[b]	Household	Household	Individual

[a]Survey funded by the British Ministry for Innovation, Research and Education
[b]Except for the 1998 survey, which covered a 3 year period
[c]The BHPS uses the same representative sample of individuals – the panel – over a period of years and interviews every adult member of sampled households every year. If a member leaves, his or her new household becomes part of the survey, likewise, new members of a household become part of the survey

---

[11]The variables used in all three Surveys are provided in the Appendix (Tables 2.9, 2.10, 2.11).

- selection of questions and resulting variables relating to the use of consumer credit;
- identification of variables considered as significant in the literature that provide a socio-demographic and economic profile of individuals using consumer credit;
- identification of one or more variables that specifically refer to individuals' financial situation in order to test whether recourse to consumer credit is motivated not only by consumption smoothing, but also by the need to manage conditions of financial difficulty.

With regards to stage one, in each of the three surveys, it is possible to establish an aggregate that represents a reasonable approximation of the total amount of consumer credit granted to households.

In the Italian survey, the head of the household is asked whether his or her household owes money from banks or other financial institutions, apart from mortgages or amounts owed for professional activities, specifically for the purchase of real assets (jewellery, gold, etc.), motor vehicles, consumer durables (furniture, electrical appliances, etc.) or non durables (holidays, fur costs, etc.).[12]

In Spain, the head of the household is asked to provide details of any other financial commitments his or her household may have apart from mortgages. Unlike the Italian survey, the EFF includes money owed for professional activities carried out in the form of family run businesses with the commitment being calculated on the total amount of the loan rather than the residual debt.[13]

In the British Household Panel Survey, respondents are asked to indicate their financial commitments, excluding secured borrowing, and provide details of, for instance, personal loans from banks and other financial institutions, overdrafts, instalment payments, credit cards, etc.[14]

In the second stage, a variety of variables were chosen that describe households' profiles and which can reasonably be expected to provide an explanation for the amounts borrowed.

---

[12]Question c31 (SHIW 2006): *"We will now talk about debts taken out to meet needs of the household and the house (do not consider debts in connection with your business). At the end of 2004 vis-à-vis banks or financial companies or for instalment payments did your household have a) debts for the purchase or restructuring of buildings? b) debts for the purchase of real goods (e.g. jewellery, gold, etc.)? c) debts for the purchase of motor vehicles (e.g. cars)? d) debts for the purchase of furniture, electrical appliances, etc? e) debts fir the purchase of non durables goods (e.g. holidays, furs, etc.) or for any other reasons? If the answer is "yes", how much in total would you say was owed on these commitments at 31stDecember 2004?"* The variable "consumer credit" was established on the basis of affirmative replies to b), c), d) and e).

[13]Question 3.1 (EFF 2005) *"How many loans other than those already mentioned do members of the household or individual firms that belong to any member of the household have? Please exclude those taken out to pay for the purchase of the main residence or other properties which have already been talked about"*. Question 3.5: *"What is the initial amount of each loan?*

[14]Questions f56 e f57 (BHPS 2005) *"I would like to ask you about any other financial commitments you may have apart from mortgages. Do you currently owe any money on the things listed on this card? hire purchase agreements, personal loans (from banks, building societies or another financial institution), credit cards, catalogue or mail order purchase agreements, DWP Social Fund loans, overdraft, student loans, any other loan from a private individual or anything else. About how much in total is owed on this/these commitments?"*.

2.3 Characteristics of Indebted Households

The variables that describe the socio-demographic and economic characteristics and conditions of respondents, which are those typically used in the literature as determinants for unsecured borrowing, are: age, educational qualifications, work status, number of household members, income and net wealth.

In the third stage, one or more qualitative variables describing a household's or individual's financial situation were identified in each survey so as to establish whether consumer credit products are used as a way of managing financial distress or for optimising intertemporal consumption.

Two variables were identified in the Italian survey: the first describes a household's financial situation, i.e. whether it manages to make ends meet, whether it manages to save or whether it has to borrow; the second describes whether household income is congruous to monthly overheads.[15]

In Spain's EFF, heads of households are asked whether during the past twelve months, their household spending was lower, the same or greater than income.[16]

Finally, the variable identified in the United Kingdom's BHPS describes an individual's economic and financial condition.[17]

For each country, we have re-processed consumer credit related data on the basis of the socio-economic variables previously mentioned and those relating to financial situation, in order to determine with regards to each of them the percentage of households holding unsecured debt.[18]

The analysis carried out is descriptive and therefore cannot capture the single contributions of individual factors, providing as it does solely an overview of the phenomenon of consumer credit and its relations with the characteristics and conditions of borrowers. Nonetheless, we feel it does raise important issues with possible implications both for the banking system and society as a whole.

---

[15]Question c29 (present only in the SHIW 2004) *"What is your household's present financial situation? We need to borrow, we need to withdraw from savings, we only just meet our budget, we manage to save a little, we manage to save a fair amount, we don't know?"* Question e12 (present from SHIW 2002 onwards) *"Is your household's disposable income enough for you to get through the month? With a great deal of difficulty, with difficulty, not easily, fairly easily, easily, very easily"*.

[16]Question 9.7 (EFF 2005) *"Would you say that over the last twelve months your household expenses have been higher, lower or the same as your income? Do not include any expenditure buying your home or any financial investment you have made"*.

[17]Question f4 (BHPS 2005) *"How well would you say you yourself are managing financially these days? Would you say you are living comfortably, doing alright, just about getting by, finding it quite difficult, find it very difficult, other?"*.

[18]The percentage was calculated making reference to each variable chosen. For instance, as regards the age variable, households were classified on the basis of the age group of the head of the household and then, for each sub-group, the percentage of households holding unsecured debt was calculated.

2.3.2 Results and Remarks

Table 2.2 shows for each country and for each survey year the percentage of households in debt along with the average amount held by them.

The first interesting aspect that emerges from the data above is the difference between countries in the proportion of households holding consumer credit.

Consistent with the macroeconomic analysis carried out in the first part of this chapter, the use of consumer credit is more widespread in the United Kingdom, with almost 32% of BHPS respondents' participating in the consumer credit market. In Italy, just over 11% of households interviewed hold this form of unsecured debt, albeit for a higher average amount (Italy: € 8,030; United Kingdom: € 6,030). Spain, which comes in between the United Kingdom and Italy as to the percentage of indebted households (2005: 20.7%), has a relatively high average amount of outstanding debt of around € 26,000. This figure, however, cannot be compared to the other two countries since, as we have already seen, personal loans also include amounts borrowed for professional or work purposes; another difference between the Spanish and Italian and UK surveys is that EFF respondents are asked to provide the full amount of the loan contracted and not the amount still to be repaid.

As regards temporal patterns emerging from the SHIW and BHPS, participation rates were broadly unchanged, whilst there were significant increases in the average unsecured debt of borrowers: in the United Kingdom, average consumer credit rose from € 3,650 in 2000 to more than € 6,000 in 2005 and in Italy the average figure increased from € 5,000 in 2000 to more than € 8,000 in 2006. In Spain there has been also a significant increase in the participation rate: from 15.5% in 2000 to 20.7% in 2005.

This increase in households' average unsecured debt reflects the growth of consumer credit at aggregate level which, as the previous macroeconomic analysis showed, has been recorded throughout Europe. The reasons for such generalised

Table 2.2 Percentage of indebted households and average amount of exposure

	Households with consumer credit (%)	Average amount (in euros)
UNITED KINGDOM		
2000	33.50	3,650
2005	31.60	6,030
ITALY		
2000	11.11	10,120,000[a]
2002	10.11	6,515
2004	12.72	6,870
2006	11.50	8,030
SPAIN		
2002	15.50	16,080
2005	20.70	25,800

[a]In Italian lira (€ 1 = ITL 1,936.27)
Source: computations on BHPS, SHIW and EFF data

2.3 Characteristics of Indebted Households

expansion stem from, on one hand, an increased propensity to debt in a macroeconomic climate of greater stability and, on the other, increased availability of credit by lenders as a result of heightened competition and improved credit risk management techniques that have made access to debt easier (Nieto 2007; Casolaro et al. 2006; Crook, Edelman, Thomas 2007).

For each household socio-demographic and economic variable we calculate the percentage of households holding consumer credit (Tables 2.3–2.5).

The results for age and education variables for the three countries are in line with Life-Cycle and Permanent Income theories: demand for credit is determined by the need on the part of households to improve lifestyle by smoothing consumption over their lifetime.[19]

Table 2.3 United Kingdom – Percentage of households with consumer credit in terms of socio-demographic and economic characteristics

	Households with consumer credit (%) 2000	2006	Number of households interviewed 2006
Age of the head			
Up to 30	47.58	41.67	3,312
31 – 40	50.90	46.47	2,608
41 – 50	43.10	37.20	2,691
51 – 65	26.76	25.85	3,273
Over 65	6.89	7.01	2,755
Work status of the head			
Employed	46.71	42.03	7,374
Self-employed	36.85	35.04	999
Unemployed	22.39	18.88	6,266
Number of household members			
1	24.68	22.71	2,136
2	30.95	28.26	4,947
3	40.95	36.53	2,814
4	41.68	38.35	2,949
More than 4	43.22	32.91	1,793
Household income			
Quartile 1	27.28	21.60	3,820
Quartile 2	30.02	26.06	3,577
Quartile 3	39.66	36.89	3,630
Quartile 4	46.80	42.52	3,612

Source: computations on BHPS data

---

[19]Demand for credit here is intended as the demand formally accepted by the financial system. The existence of potential demand rejected by lenders does not appear in the surveys; the inclusion of such information could produce a demand variable that differs from country-to-country and from one period to another.

Table 2.4 Italy – Percentage of households with consumer credit in terms of socio-demographic and economic characteristics

	Households with consumer credit (%)				Number of households interviewed
	2000	2002	2004	2006	2006
Age of the head					
Up to 30	21.47	15.46	22.87	18.99	237
31 – 40	18.54	18.72	21.35	17.97	1,007
41 – 50	16.60	16.13	21.85	17.22	1,504
51 – 65	10.18	9.63	12.54	13.69	2,338
Over 65	2.08	2.64	2.84	3.29	2,676
Education of the head					
No qualifications	2.31	3.51	4.70	2.56	429
Primary school	6.71	5.38	6.55	6.46	2,060
Middle school	13.92	13.48	15.21	14.27	2,187
High school	15.29	13.56	18.26	14.06	2,397
University degree	10.86	11.34	13.42	14.51	689
Work status of the head					
Employed	17.68	16.99	20.91	17.81	2,707
Self-employed	14.73	15.57	17.98	16.12	794
Unemployed	5.95	5.02	6.93	6.64	4,261
Number of household members					
1	5.36	5.05	6.47	5.46	1,923
2	7.10	6.90	8.59	9.05	2,364
3	13.56	12.45	17.80	15.67	1,653
4	17.46	15.05	20.12	17.29	1,822
More than 4	13.21	17.43	17.58	5.46	1,923
					3,662
Household income					
Quartile 1	5.26	5.79	7.49	6.10	1,967
Quartile 2	10.50	8.94	11.17	10.04	1,923
Quartile 3	13.83	13.14	16.67	13.70	1,963
Quartile 4	14.98	12.71	16.22	16.29	1,909
Household net wealth					
Quartile 1	13.36	12.45	15.25	13.97	1,969
Quartile 2	9.70	8.07	12.94	10.41	1,921
Quartile 3	10.96	10.57	10.59	10.89	1,883
Quartile 4	10.41	9.31	12.25	10.71	1,989

Source: computations on SHIW data

Amounts borrowed in the form of consumer credit are, in fact, for the most part concentrated amongst younger households, which borrow in order to guarantee uniform levels of spending over their lifetimes and, consequently, to improve lifestyles (Crook 2006; Fabbri and Padula 2004; Magri 2007). In particular, the

2.3 Characteristics of Indebted Households

Table 2.5 Spain – Percentage of households with consumer credit in terms of socio-demographic and economic characteristics

	Households with consumer credit (%)		Number of households interviewed
	2002	2005	2005
Age of the head			
Up to 35	26.54	33.14	519
35 – 44	26.29	32.51	889
45 – 54	27.01	32.04	1,108
55 – 64	19.90	21.98	1,210
65 – 74	8.21	9.88	1,316
Over 74	2.30	2.72	920
Education of the head			
No qualifications	9.91	6.36	173
Primary school	14.54	16.09	1,895
Middle school	20.99	28.56	970
High school	21.65	25.76	1,351
University degree	16.55	18.82	1,573
Work status of the head			
Employed	25.52	32.74	2,181
Self-employed	23.17	25.58	825
Unemployed	11.05	10.55	2,956
Number of household members			
1	6.14	9.12	1,042
2	11.35	13.69	2,009
3	21.24	26.02	1,318
4	25.97	31.75	1,118
More than 4	31.76	35.58	475
Household income			
Quartile 1	8.28	12.20	1,483
Quartile 2	17.93	23.24	1,493
Quartile 3	22.83	27.39	1,475
Quartile 4	20.57	20.19	1,511
Household net wealth			
Quartile 1	21.88	29.24	1,491
Quartile 2	18.22	23.68	1,402
Quartile 3	15.92	16.87	1,583
Quartile 4	12.82	13.59	1,486

Source: computations on EFF data

percentage of households' holding debt peaks, in Italy, when the head of the household is under the age of 30, in the United Kingdom between the ages of 30 and 40, whilst in Spain the percentage remains substantially unchanged until the age of 55.

Educational qualifications also confirm the supposition that a higher level of education is a robust proxy of rising future earnings and is therefore positively correlated to the amount of debt contracted (Grant 2003; Del Rio, Young 2005a). In Italy and Spain, where data are available, the percentage of individuals with personal loans is higher amongst the medium/high education groups. In particular, in both countries the proportion of borrowers with a degree or post-graduate qualification increases over time, as does the level of financial education necessary to access and select financial products effectively.

The net wealth variable is also consistent with the empirical analyses discussed in Chap 1. The percentage of households holding consumer credit is higher amongst those households with lower levels of net wealth. This confirms the results reported in the literature that show higher wealth levels allow households to satisfy their needs without resorting to debt (Magri 2007; Del Rio and Young 2005a). In Italy and Spain, where data are available, the percentage of borrowers peaks at the first quartile.

The income variable is also in line with findings presented in the literature (Crook 2006; Fabbri and Padula 2004): the percentage of individuals holding unsecured debt rises with higher incomes. In particular, in the United Kingdom and Italy, the proportion of individuals with debt commitments reaches a peak for individuals and households at the fourth income quartile, whilst in Spain at the third quartile. Higher income levels are probably less volatile, a fact that leads to increases from both the credit supply and demand sides.

As regards employment status in all three countries the employed hold the highest levels of debt. This could stem from the fact that employees' wage packets offer banks considerable advantages in this otherwise unsecured form of lending: in addition to *ex ante* guarantees represented by the salary itself, banks can debit directly amounts owed, whilst using the current account as an effective vehicle to promote and distribute other retail services.

In this analysis, financial conditions variables flank others typically used in the literature with the specific aim of investigating the possibility that debt is contracted not only to allow individuals to smooth consumption over the life cycle, but also at least in some cases, to face conditions of financial stress (Tables 2.6–2.8).

Interestingly, the variables describing households' financial situations have a significant influence on participation in the consumer credit market.

In Italy, the percentage of debtors in financially critical or quite critical conditions is, respectively, 10.9% and 13.3%. Higher still is the proportion of households with debt that declare their incomes do not allow them to get to the end of the month (27.5%). Also in Spain, participation in the credit market is high amongst individuals who claim their earnings do not allow them to cover expenses (31.4%) and rises compared to 2002, with the percentage being higher for non owner-occupiers living in rented accommodation in comparison to home owners. The highest percentage, however, is in the United Kingdom, where 49.3% of borrowers declare themselves to be in situations of financial difficulty.

2.3 Characteristics of Indebted Households

Table 2.6 United Kingdom – Percentage of households with consumer credit in terms of financial situation

	Households with consumer credit (%)		Number of households interviewed
	2000	2006	2006
Financial condition			
Living comfortably	26.67	23.16	4,438
Doing alright	37.31	33.12	5,827
Just about getting by	38.20	35.61	3,384
Finding it difficult	46.82	48.05	668
Finding it very difficult	51.84	49.31	290
Don't know	9.52	23.16	4,438

Source: computations on BHPS data

Table 2.7 Italy – Percentage of households with consumer credit in terms of financial situation

	Households with consumer credit (%)			Number of households interviewed
	2002	2004	2006	2006
Financial situation				
Have to borrow	n.a.	27.46	n.a.	
Have to use savings	n.a.	13.66	n.a.	
Just about getting by	n.a.	12.32	n.a.	
Manage to save something	n.a.	12.59	n.a.	
Manage to save quite a bit	n.a.	8.71	n.a.	
Don't know	n.a.	3.37	n.a.	
General economic condition				
Difficult	10.24	13.49	10.94	2,276
Quite difficult	10.51	13.50	13.33	2,566
Quite comfortable	9.48	11.68	10.44	2,156
Comfortable	10.49	10.93	10.08	764

Source: computations on SHIW data

These data show that there is also a section of the population that have to borrow in order to manage their household finances. This evidence alone does not conflict with standard life-cycle intertemporal optimisation, but it certainly draws attention to the fact that parts of outstanding debt contracted through consumer credit forms are held by households and individuals that, in the event of an unexpected negative variation in income, may find themselves in a situation of over-indebtedness. Support for this position is provided by the fact that in all three countries a not insignificant percentage of debtors is aged over 65, typically a period in life when borrowing cannot be justified by expectations of rising future income. Similarly, a statistically significant number of unemployed and low-income[20] individuals hold debt.

---

[20]Low-income individuals belong to the first income quartile, with the following maximum income levels per country: United Kingdom – GBP 5,000; Italy – euro 14,000; Spain – euro 14,000. The category "unemployed" includes also the retired.

Table 2.8 Spain – Percentage of households with consumer credit in terms of financial situation

	Households with consumer credit (%)		Number of households interviewed
	2002	2005	2005
Accommodation			
Rented	19.06	28.99	576
Owned	16.69	19.27	5,008
Other	23.18	27.78	378
General condition			
Spending is greater than income	25.71	31.35	858
Spending is less than income	14.79	16.73	2,194
Spending is the same as income	16.10	20.65	2,910

Source: computations on EFF data

The results discussed so far confirm that participation in the credit market is predominantly motivated by the need on the part of households, according to their specific characteristics and conditions, to use debt, in accordance with life-cycle theories, to distribute income and spending over time as a way of guaranteeing greater economic welfare.[21] However, a group of households exists with lower levels of income and net wealth and less stable financial situations that use consumer credit as a means of making ends meet.

The analysis carried out in this work has shown that the average amount of unsecured debt has risen over time. Consequently, it can reasonably be hypothesised that if this debt were tending to be concentrated amongst financially weaker households, over-indebtedness would be the inevitable result as individuals would find it difficult to respect their commitments on the basis of current income.

This descriptive analysis does not allow us to empirically test this hypothesis. However, the question is being addressed by an increasing number of researchers equipped with appropriate economic models and econometric solutions. The results that emerge form these studies appear to confirm the hypothesis that unsecured debt is becoming concentrated amongst particular social groups – households with low income, low wealth or an already high debt-income ratio – which run the risk of over-indebtedness because of their vulnerability to adverse events, such as a fall in income or higher debt repayment charges following an interest-rate hike (Del Rio and Young 2005b; Rinaldi and Sanchez-Arellano 2006; May et al. 2004; Cavalletti et al. 2008).

This situation needs to be addressed both by the banking system, for the negative consequences that over-indebtedness can have on banks' retail lending portfolios, and by policy makers and governments, for the social and economic repercussions that over-indebtedness can have for the society.

---

[21] According to the standard Life-Cycle theory, the demand for credit should be made on the basis of increased expected incomes and should, as a result, be higher amongst young people and those with high educational qualifications as these individuals forecast higher future income flows. Similarly, demand for credit should be higher amongst individuals with higher job status and/or higher current income as these will enjoy easier access to the credit market.

Appendix

Table 2.9 Variables used from SHIW

DEBITB	Debts for tangible goods
DEBITC	Debts for motor vehicles
DEBITD	Debts for furniture, household appliances
DEBITE	Debts for non-durable goods
TDEBITB...E	Amount of debt
CLETA	Age
NCOMP	Number of persons living in the household
STUDIO	Educational qualification
QUAL	Employment status
Y	Income
W	Net wealth
SITFIN	Financial situation
CONDGEN	Economic condition

Table 2.10 Variables used from EFF

p1_5_1	Level of education
np1	Number of person in the household
p2_1	Ownership status
Bage	Age
Pperso	Amount of personal debt
ptmos_tarj	Amount of credit card debt
Potrasd	Amount of other personal debt
Nsitlabdom	Employment situation
p9_7	Economic and financial situation
Riquezanet	Net wealth
renthog04€05	Income

Table 2.11 Variables used from BHPS

ODEBT	Currently owe money:
ODEBTA	– On hire purchase
ODEBTB	– On personal loan
ODEBTC	– On credit card
ODEBTD	– On mail order purchase
ODEBTE	– On DWP Social Fund loan
ODEBTF	– On loans from individuals
ODEBTG	– On something else
ODEBTH	– On overdraft
ODEBTI	– On student loan
ODEBJB	How much
OAGE	Age
OHHSIZE	Number of person in the household
OJBSTAT	Current income activity
OFIST	Financial situation
OFIYR	Annual income

Chapter 3
The Profitability of the Consumer Credit Industry

3.1 Introduction

The strong growth recorded by the consumer credit sector over recent years has undoubtedly been driven by rising demand on the part of individuals and households for unsecured debt solutions. Nevertheless, the supply side has also played a significant role in this process: consumer credit financial intermediaries have shown the ability to respond to market needs by developing and distributing innovative products and raising service standard levels. These moves have been accompanied by attempts to optimise asset portfolio sizes in order both to generate the economies of scale necessary for the containment of the administrative and management costs associated with the supply of large numbers of small loans as well as to create adequately diversified loan portfolios.

In this chapter, we analyse the consumer credit industry with a specific focus on the types of players, their lending policies and their profitability. To valuate the sector's profitability, data from the financial statements of a sample of French, German, Italian and Spanish consumer credit companies will be examined.

Emphasis on profitability is justified by the particular characteristics of the consumer credit industry. In fact, the rapid growth in consumer credit in Europe described in the previous chapter has been tracked by increasing levels of market complexity and competitiveness, which have certainly left their mark on earnings margins and portfolio risk levels. A comparative analysis of performances recorded by consumer credit providers from four different European Member States is also useful in the light of the opportunities for integration and expansion offered by implementation into domestic legislation of the new Consumer Credit Directive.

3.2 The Consumer Credit Industry: Main Features

3.2.1 *Consumer Credit Lenders*

The provision of consumer credit can be categorised on the basis of the lender's level of specialisation.

An initial distinction can be made, on one hand, between universal banks offering a broad range of financial services and, on the other, consumer credit companies (CCCs). The latter, in turn, can be sub-divided into:

– Specialised financial intermediaries belonging to banking or financial groups
– Captive companies fully owned by manufacturing or retail groups

Universal banks providing many types of retail and corporate products, including consumer credit, are typically commercial banks which, as part of their traditional banking activity, offer lending products both to corporate and retail customers.[1]

Specialised financial intermediaries, conversely, focus exclusively on lending to households and, in particular, the offer of consumer credit.

Captive companies are financial companies that also limit their activity to consumer credit, but the amounts advanced are destined exclusively to the purchase of the parent company's product. Captives, in this role, provide dealers not only with a service that can play a crucial role in consumers' purchasing decisions, but also one that creates and consolidates customer loyalty.

It is important to point out that the distinctions made between universal banks, specialised financial intermediaries and captive companies, however, reflect the level of economic specialisation on the part of the lender and its ownership nature. Conversely, as regards the ownership structure, many lenders in the consumer credit industry are linked by a series of cross holdings. Major banking groups, in fact, not only provide customers with consumer credit as part of their normal banking activities, but also via specialised banks with distinct legal identity or dedicated finance companies. Furthermore, in many cases banking groups enter into agreements with manufacturers and retailers.[2]

Moreover, consumer credit lending from different types of financial intermediaries reflect a market segmentation according to which universal banks concentrate mainly on lending directly to their customers, captive companies provide loans linked to the purchase of specific products, whilst other specialised finance

---

[1] Consumer credit belongs evidently to banks' retail product portfolios. However, in some local contexts (above all in the case of the New Entrants to the EU discussed in Chap. 2, Sect. 2.2.3), consumer credit is used by owners of small businesses and the self-employed, such as craft workers, artisans, professionals, whose personal and professional financial needs are closely interrelated.

[2] Credit Agricole, for example, owns outright Sofinco, Frances's leading consumer credit specialist, which provides consumer credit via a series of joint ventures with major retailers (Auchan and Tesco) and car manufacturers (Renault and Fiat).

3.2 The Consumer Credit Industry: Main Features

intermediaries offer a wide range of consumer credit products and services across both areas.

In a context of market segmentation, it is worthwhile pointing out that alongside mainstream credit providers (universal banks and CCCs), in some local contexts other lenders exist that specifically target the sub-prime market. This segment is made up by individuals and households which, due to low income and/or low credit rating and the related costs and risks, find it difficult to access mainstream channels. In the United Kingdom, for instance, pawnbrokers[3] and doorstep lenders are relatively common.

The former provide short-term credit, usually for only few weeks, against pledged goods that are returned to the borrower on repayment of the loan. Doorstep lenders, as the name suggests, lend and collect repayments door to door. These moneylenders generally operate on a small scale although large, national networks also exist.[4] These lenders, by offering the quick supply of small sums of money, meet the needs of a category of borrower that represents little or no incentive for mainstream credit providers.

Borrowing costs, however, are high and borrowers, when unable to meet repayment obligations, are forced to extend the life of the loan, so increasing their interest and commission commitments (Skiba, Tobacman 2008; Kempson 2002; Consumer Affairs Victoria 2006). In the United Kingdom, since no statutory interest-rate ceiling exists, the cost of these types of loans would, in other countries, be considered as usury. It has to be said, however, that in markets where loans ceilings are in place, borrowers in difficulty with loans owed to formal credit suppliers often resort to informal or illegal lenders, i.e. loan sharks.[5]

3.2.2 Consumer Credit Products

The range of consumer credit products can be divided into two main categories on the basis of what the funds are used for[6]:

- Loans linked to a specific purchase (vehicle and point of sale financing)
- Loans not linked to a specific purchase

The first category refers to loans granted for the purchase of specific items, such as motor cars, furniture, electrical appliances and high-tech products. In recent

---

[3] Members belong to the National Pawnbrokers Association, whose business is subject to the provisions of the Consumer Credit Act of 1974.
[4] For instance, Cattles and London and Provident Financial.
[5] For differences in Europe regarding the presence of loan ceilings, see Chap. 4 and Sect. 4.3.6 in particular.
[6] The analysis that follows will concentrate on mainstream credit providers.

years, targeted lending has been extended to other sectors such as healthcare, fitness and health centres (Assofin 2007, ASF 2007).

The contract in this category of loan is signed with the customer directly at the point of sale and the lender is either the captive of the parent company (particularly in the car and retail sectors[7]) or a specialised finance company working in agreement with a merchant or dealer.

Universal banks tend to concentrate on consumer credit which is not linked to specific purchases, an area in which also specialised finance intermediaries are active.[8]

Figure 3.1 shows the distribution of outstanding consumer credit loans by loan type in major European markets at year-end 2006.

Interestingly, significant differences exist between countries: on one hand, there are markets, such as France and the United Kingdom, in which demand and supply

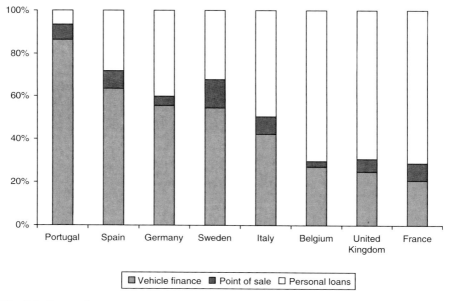

Fig. 3.1 Outstanding consumer credit by loan type (%, 2006)
Source: computations on Eurofinas data

---

[7] The principal European players in the car finance sector are BMW, Fiat, Renault and General Motors, whilst the major captives belonging to major retailers are Carrefour, El Corte Ingles, Lafayette, Groupe Casino.

[8] In Italy, for example, in 2006 amounts lent by universal banks accounted for 11% of their consumer credit totals, with the remaining amount being for non-specific purchases (personal loans, credit cards, salary-backed loans). As regards specialised finance companies, specific and non-specific loan shares are more evenly balanced at 55 and 45%, respectively (Assofin 2007).

are principally for credits not linked to the purchase of specific goods or services, whilst, on the other, there are countries, such as Portugal and Spain, where specific purchase-targeted lending dominates.

The first group of countries is characterised by the extensive use of consumer credit by individuals and households and substantial market maturity; in the second group of countries, considerable room for growth in the industry remains.

However, as Fig. 3.2 clearly shows, there is an expansionary trend in the non-specific segment in all countries.

This growth reflects changes both on the demand and supply sides of the market.

With regards to the demand for consumer credit, we saw in Chap 2 how expansion was most evident in comparatively immature markets, such as Italy. In particular, households and individuals are increasingly prepared to use debt to finance their consumption needs, with the positive effects this tendency has had on demand for consumer credit. Additionally, financial knowledge levels amongst consumers have risen not only as regards saving and investment, but also in the area of borrowing. This has led, consequently, to greater demand for loans granted directly by lenders rather than via dealers or merchants at the point of sale.[9]

On the supply side, in addition to the demand-driven factors outlined above that have pushed lenders to focus increasingly on this area, growth in the consumer credit industry has also been the result of heightened competition and resulting tighter margins in addition to innovation both in product design and credit risk management.

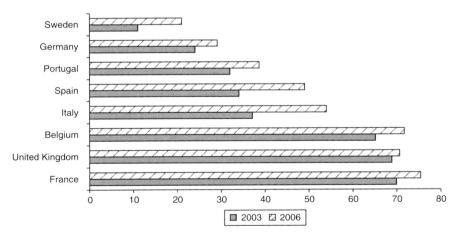

Fig. 3.2 Non-specific purchase loans as a percentage of new loans (%, 2003–2006)
Source: computations on Eurofinas data

---

[9]For a detailed analysis of changes taking place on domestic consumer markets, for Italy, see Assofin (2007), for Spain, Banco de Espana (2007), for France, ASF (2007), and for other major European countries OEE (2005).

These changes have contributed to an overhaul of product portfolios in the search for cost containments in distribution, expansion of potential customer bases to exploit cross selling opportunities and heightened effectiveness of customer loyalty programmes.

In particular, in recent years, there have been significant increases in the use of revolving credit cards on the back of strong growth in payment systems (ATMs and POS) and card usage. Further expansion is likely with the creation of SEPA – Single Euro Payment Area – and the shared infrastructure, standardised procedures and raised security levels it foresees.[10]

Revolving credit cards are an attractive form of lending for banks as they generate commission revenues associated with charge cards (annual fees, fixed charges, merchant and interchange fees) and as well as interest income owed on instalment repayments.[11] Cards also provide, by monitoring customer spending, useful information for lenders to improve their cross-selling opportunities. Finally, credit cards are suitable for the development of co-branding agreements aimed at increasing potential customer numbers.[12]

In addition to a generalised move in credit flows to non-specific purchases and the continuing expansion of revolving credit, lenders are refining product portfolios to satisfy specific market segments in order both to satisfy more effectively existing customer needs and to develop specific market niches, such as age-based segments.

Older age groups in fact account for a not insignificant share of demand for consumer credit (see Sect. 2.3.2). Such demand is apparently in contrast with the life-cycle theory, which holds that demand for credit tends to fall with age as individuals become better-placed to finance their needs from own resources (see Sect. 1.2). The reasons for demand for credit also amongst senior customer segments probably lies with the fact that, on one hand, older individuals prefer to finance spending by borrowing so as to keep wealth levels accumulated over their lifetime intact for their children ("intergenerational transfer"), whilst, on the other, older age groups can access credit on behalf of children or other family members

---

[10] The principles, rules and best practices established by the European Payment Council (EPC) and agreed on at interbank level are contained in the SEPA Framework Card. On implementation by banks and credit circuits, European customers will be able to use cash cards for payments and withdrawals through SEPA at the same terms and conditions applied at national level. The EPC's objective is to create a payment area free from legal, commercial or technological barriers restricting harmonisation in card usage (EPC, 2006).

[11] Credit cards are classified as either charge or revolving, depending on the method of repayment. Amounts owed on charge cards are settled in one payment, typically in the following month. No interest is charged in the period between use and repayment. Revolving cards, however, are linked to a revolving credit line that allows the card holder to repay in instalments the amounts owed. A detailed economic and technical analysis of credit cards, the production process and the performance profiles of the credit card industry can be found in Vandone (2001).

[12] Lenders' revenues from such agreements are, however, uncertain in comparison to the investments a partnership agreement requires. A key factor lenders have to therefore evaluate is the size of the commercial partners' customer base.

3.2 The Consumer Credit Industry: Main Features

who, because of their employment status (i.e. unemployed or in temporary employment), have a high credit-risk profile.

As regards young people, credit forms are for instance targeted at students to cover university fees and related living costs,[13] which will be repaid either at the end of the period of study or when the borrower starts to earn a salary. Student loans have been an important part of banks' personal lending strategies for several years in the United Kingdom, where the consumer credit market is more developed and customer segmentation more advanced than in other countries. Concerns, however, exist about the current levels of student debt in the United Kingdom and the impact these may have on young adults in the early stages of their working lives.

Consolidation of loans represents an addition to lenders' product portfolios. Borrowers with various loan liabilities can consolidate the single positions into a sole exposure at a longer maturity thereby, typically, enabling a fixed rate and more manageable monthly repayment instalments. Loan consolidation is widespread in the United States and is becoming increasingly more common in the highly competitive UK market.

The range of consumer credit products is often complemented by loyalty and flexible repayment packages[14] and above all by Payment Protection Insurance.[15] This form of insurance produces a cascade of positive externalities for lenders in the form of fees generated by a product which, as part of the loan package, has contained costs; insurance also lowers risk levels which, in turn, reduce the likelihood of credit recovery or impairment charges. Positive externalities are also enjoyed by society as a whole in the form of welfare cost savings arising from reduced exposure to financial risks for individuals and households in the face of negative unexpected events. With these externalities in mind, Payment

---

[13] Student loans are particularly common in the United States, where university and college fees are extremely high (Salmi 2000; Ziederman 2002, Payne and Callendar 1997).

[14] Cetelem (BNP Paribas) has created "eco-friendly" loans linked to the purchase of goods (e.g. electrical appliances) with low environmental impact, low consumption and high energy saving levels. CartaSi', Italy's principal credit card operator, has developed a single card which offers two lines of credit: one to cover everyday expenses and one for unexpected or extraordinary purchases. Repayment on the first is either on a single charge or instalment basis, whilst the second credit line offers solely instalment repayments on the amount advanced over the normal credit limit offered by the card. The product also offers flexible repayment terms, such as the possibility of temporarily suspending repayments, along with text updates of transactions performed and instalments due.

[15] Payment Protection Insurance (PPI) is a scheme that seeks to provide consumers with debt repayment cover in the case of an unexpected event, such as redundancy, illness or death. Details regarding the objectives and features of the scheme can be found at www.money-madeclear.fsa.gov.uk. A recent report by Britain's Competition Commission (2008) reveals that the high commission charges paid by consumers for these forms of insurance products are essentially the result of lack of competition. For instance, PPI is offered by lenders together with the loan granted, but most consumers are unaware that payment protection cover can be bought separately.

Protection Insurance is compulsory for certain lending products.[16] Payment protection also acts as an effective vehicle for penetrating relatively high-risk market segments thanks to the fact that the loan granted is fully secured.

Finally, the retail and delivery approach adopted can work as an effective means of exploiting market potential, reducing transaction times and enhancing multi-channel strategies.[17] Internet use, in particular, is rapidly growing not only as a showcase for lenders' services and products, but also as a distribution channel in its own right.[18]

3.3 Profitability Analysis of a Sample of Specialised Consumer Credit Companies

3.3.1 Objectives and Methodology

As a result of the growth of the consumer credit industry in Europe in recent years, allied to forecasts for its continuing expansion in many European markets, an analysis of the profitability of consumer credit companies can provide a useful contribution to work in the area of consumer credit.

In this section, we will analyse the performances of a sample of CCCs, both specialised financial intermediaries and captives, in order to show any differences in profitability present in the four markets under investigation – France, Germany, Italy and Spain[19] – and identify the causes for these differences.

To this end we first calculate the profitability of single lenders using the profitability indicator ratio Return on Assets (ROA),[20] defined as net income divided by

---

[16] In Italy, for example, in the case of *"cessione del quinto"* loans, Presidential Decree 180/50 foresees mandatory cover for lenders in the event of death or job loss.

[17] MPS has launched a new line of personal loans – *"Prs Carattere"* – with rapid approval times and competitive terms. Cetelem is the leading internet provider of consumer credit in France, followed by Sofinco.

[18] See Banque de France (2008).

[19] The decision to focus an analysis of profitability on these four countries is due to the fact that, although they are amongst the largest in Europe in terms of credit outstandings, the extent of consumer credit use and the speed of market growth differ (see Chap 2, Sect. 2.2.1 and 2.2.2). In particular, Spain, Germany and France have consumer credit/GDP ratios above the European average, whilst Italy is well below, though catching up fast. Moreover, in recent years, consumer credit debt levels in Spain have risen to an extent that the country's consumer credit/GDP ratio is now higher the France's, while in Germany the country's consumer credit/GDP ratio is slightly reducing. The analysis examines therefore four fundamentally different markets: France is mature with contained rates of growth but still dynamic; Spain is a relatively young market, but with high levels of both credit card use and growth; Germany is a market of considerable dimension but static; Italy is an immature, but rapidly growing market.

[20] Return on Equity (ROE, defined as net income divided by total equity) was not used as this indicator is influenced, above all in cross-country analyses, by different levels of company capitalisation. Details regarding the choice of indicator and variables used in the analysis are given in later paragraphs.

total assets. Subsequently, in order to identify factors determining cross-country differences, we broke down ROA into the five following ratios[21]:

$$\text{ROA} = \frac{\text{NP}}{\text{BT}} * \frac{\text{BT}}{\text{OP}} * \frac{\text{OP}}{\text{TR}} * \frac{\text{TR}}{\text{NI}} * \frac{\text{NI}}{\text{TA}}$$

The rationale for the schema above has been widely discussed in the literature.[22] In fact, the metric ROA in this form shows firstly the impact on the result of a raft of factors and secondly how effectively a company manages them: tax, non-recurring items, operating costs, ability to generate non-interest revenues and interest margins.

In reality, the first two factors cannot be seen as being part of an active strategic approach adopted by consumer credit suppliers: tax essentially leaves little room for manoeuvre, whilst extraordinary factors, though possibly having a significant effect on a period's results, do not characterise an operating environment. Nonetheless, these two factors may have considerable explanatory value when performing cross-country and cross-industry analyses, for example in the case of a period of discontinuity in a lender's results.

The intercurrent relation between ROA and the variables explaining variations in it will be analysed by using a linear regression model.

3.3.2 *The Sample*

The sample is made up by 86 consumer credit companies: 21 from France, 27 from Germany, 21 from Italy and 17 from Spain.

All the companies are members of their respective national associations.[23] In particular, for each country, lenders were categorised on the basis of size and ownership structure. The resulting sample made up by large-sized consumer credit companies, both belonging to banking groups ("finance companies") and to manufacturing or retailing groups ("captives").

Information and data used in the analysis were taken from the Bureau van Dijk's Bankscope database. For companies not included in this database,[24] the official financial statements, accessible from the Euridile platform, were used.

The analysis concentrated on the years 2005 and 2006, the first two to be impacted by the adoption of IAS/IFRS. The use of national GAAP prior to 2005 and the absence of comparatives that differing national standards entail made a longer time horizon unworkable.

---

[21] NP: Net profit; BT: Profit before tax; OP: Operating profit; TR: Total operating revenues; NI: Net interest income; TA: Total assets.

[22] See Saunders and Cornett (2007).

[23] France: *Association Francaise des Societés Financières* (ASF); Germany: *Bankenfachverband*; Italy: *Associazione Italiana del Credito al Consumo e Immobiliare* (ASSOFIN); Spain: *Asociacion National de Establecimientos Financieros de Credito* (ASNEF).

[24] These companies are for the most part brand lenders whose data are not always available in the Bankscope database, but whose inclusion provides important information for the analysis with relation to the ownership nature.

Unconsolidated company statements were used to examine the specificities of consumer credit operations carried out in one country rather than the activities of any foreign subsidiary or associated companies operating in other sectors, related or otherwise. For this reason, universal banks were not included in the sample and consequently consumer credit amounts granted by them. The inclusion of universal banks with considerable operational differences (and the absence of comparatives this implied) would otherwise have impaired the significance of the results.

The sample is highly representative of the outstanding consumer credit granted by specialised lenders, accounting for, at year-end 2006, 74% of the total for France, 96% for Germany, 88% for Italy and 81% for Spain. Table 3.1 shows also the overall figure of consumer credit outstandings in each country both by universal banks and specialised lenders. The figures referring to universal banks are shown in order to provide a picture of the size of the national market.[25] However, as mentioned above, the analysis concentrated exclusively on CCCs as only these companies provide financial and economic results relating specifically to consumer credit activities.[26] Table 3.2 illustrates the composition of the

Table 3.1 Sample representativeness: consumer credit outstandings (millions of euros, 2006)

	Outstanding consumer credit	Market share
FRANCE		
Sample	52,341	73.69%
Consumer credit companies (CCCs)	71,028	
(Universal banks and CCCs)	(148,748)	
GERMANY		
Sample	69,668	95.93%
CCCs	72,620	
(Universal banks and CCCs)	(228,400)	
ITALY		
Sample	64,834	88.09%
CCCs	73,596	
(Universal banks and CCCs)	(85,630)	
SPAIN		
Sample	24,846	80.46%
CCCs	30,879	
(Universal banks and CCCs)	(92,213)	

Source: Eurofinas for CCCs' total consumer credit outstandings and National Central Banks for overall amounts granted by domestic financial systems

---

[25] In Italy, consumer credit is for the most part provided by specialised lenders, whilst in Spain and even more so in Germany, the market is dominated by universal banks.

[26] The same reasons explain the exclusion from the sample of finance companies offering diversified financial services in the area of operative leases, finance leases and/or factoring. Other companies were excluded from the sample due to the absence of financial statements for one of the 2 years under analysis.

3.3 Profitability Analysis of a Sample of Specialised Consumer Credit Companies 55

Table 3.2 Composition of the sample (millions of euros, 2006)

	Number	Total assets Average	Total assets Median	Total assets Standard deviation	Finance companies (% total assets)	Captives (% total assets)
France	21	4,033	1,824	5,966	70.47	29.53
Germany	27	2,964	1,254	4,894	38.29	61.74
Italy	21	3,556	3,048	2,475	78.88	21.12
Spain	17	2,647	1,584	4,322	79.16	20.84

sample,[27] whilst details of the companies including their type (finance companies or captive, national or foreign) are given in the Appendix at Table 3.10.[28]

3.3.3 Main Results

Consumer credit companies' earning sources are interest income – the primary source of earnings – and non-interest revenues. The contribution of commission income has increased in recent years thanks to a wider range of products and services and heightened attention to market segmentation and customer loyalty programmes. Significant examples of non-interest income sources are the various forms of commission collected on revolving credit cards (annual, merchant and interchange fees) and earnings on the supply of other loan-linked products, such as Payment Protection Insurance (OEE 2005, Weill 2004).

The principal cost items are interest charges on funding and commissions payable to retail points of sale through which specific-purchase loans are channelled. Other costs include operating overheads and impairment charges related to the quality of loan portfolios.

A firm's profitability is typically measured by the indicators indicators ROE and ROA. The first, calculated as net income over total equity, shows how much profit a company earned on each euro invested by its shareholders; the second, calculated as net income over total assets, is an indicator of how profitable a firm is relative to its total assets, measuring the net profit generated for each euro of net assets.

Since ROE is inevitably linked to a company's level of capitalisation, ROA, which measures the profitability of invested capital, is better-equipped in a cross-country analysis of companies with different levels and types of financial leverage (Athanasoglou et al. 2005). Also with this metric, however, in carrying out

---

[27] In Germany, where universal banks dominate the consumer credit supply side, specialised consumer credit companies have a limited presence and those active are mainly captives.

[28] The sample is not balanced on a country basis as this would have limited the possibility of including the most important companies in each country.

Table 3.3 The average ROA (%, 2006)

	2005	2006
France	1.34***	1.37***
Germany	0.41***	0.41***
Italy	0.97***	0.64***
Spain	1.23***	1.25***

One-way Anova was used to test for differences among the four countries. The symbols *, ** and *** indicate significance at 10%, 5% and 1%. The test results are given in the appendix (Table 3.11)

a comparison of similar companies it has to be remembered that total assets and therefore ROA can be impacted by the securitisation of part of the loan portfolio.

As regards the sample under examination, gearing levels for 2006 in the four countries in fact differ with average total assets/shareholder equity ratios of 12, 14, 20 and 11 for France, Germany, Italy and Spain, respectively.[29] The robustness of ROA as a yardstick for cross-country profitability analysis, appears confirmed by the fact that securitisation levels in the four countries are similar.[30]

Table 3.3 shows the average ROA of the specialised consumer credit providers in each country.[31]

Figures for 2006 show that the average ROA in each of the four countries differs significantly in statistical terms. In particular, the average ROA for Germany (0.41%) and Italy (0.64%) is considerably lower than averages recorded for Spain (1.25%) and France (1.37%) and, for Italy, markedly down on 2005. The fall in profitability recorded by Italian CCCs from 2005 to 2006 has been reported by

---

[29] One-way Anova was used to test for differences among the four countries. The symbols *, ** and *** indicate significance at 10%, 5% and 1%. As regards financial leverage, differences are significant at 1% for 2005 and 10% for 2006.

[30] Securitisation levels are substantially similar in all the countries. In fact, the Italian Consumer Credit Association ASSOFIN reports an increased use of securitisation by consumer credit companies: at the end of June 2007, 14.1% of gross consumer credit balances had been securitised, the majority of which relating to vehicle finance (Assofin 2007). Similar securitisation rates – 15% – were recorded for 2006 in Spain (Banco de Espana 2007), whilst in France at year-end 2003, 11.4% of gross consumer credit balances had been securitised (Banque de France 2004). In the case of Germany, it is not possible to identify the share of loan portfolios securitised by consumer credit suppliers. However, as the sample is principally made up by captives, it can reasonably be supposed that this figure is not higher than that recorded for other countries in the sample referring as it does mainly to transactions performed by financial intermediaries belonging to banking groups.

[31] ROA performance comparatives of the overall banking sector in the four countries, as provided by the International Monetary Fund's Financial Soundness Indicators, are as follows: France 0.6%, Germany 0.8%, Italy 0.8%, Spain 0.9% (IMF 2007). Average ROA for consumer credit companies in France and Spain is markedly higher than figures recorded for each country's banking industry, whereas this is not the case for Germany and Italy. Reasons for this situation will be given later in the chapter.

3.3 Profitability Analysis of a Sample of Specialised Consumer Credit Companies 57

Table 3.4 A breakdown of the ROA (%, 2006)

	NP/BT	BT/OP	OP/TR	TR/NI	NI/TA
FRANCE					
2005	56.38*	97.03***	27.75	122.70	5.90
2006	69.59***	106.61***	26.72	125.00**	5.58**
GERMANY					
2005	42.60*	56.71***	23.18	176.86	4.10
2006	37.87***	39.05***	18.45	175.45**	3.96**
ITALY					
2005	62.92*	163.29***	28.31	120.89	3.81
2006	54.17***	106.29***	29.19	130.55**	3.07**
SPAIN					
2005	81.24*	104.11***	32.06	126.16	4.45
2006	64.06***	107.63***	32.16	123.88**	4.46**

One-way Anova was used to test for differences among the four countries. The symbols *, ** and *** indicate significance at 10%, 5% and 1%. The test results are given in the appendix (Table 3.11)
NP Net profit; *BT* Profit before tax; *OP* Operating profit; *TR* Total operating revenues; *NI* Net interest income; *TA* Total assets

Ossfin (2007) and is put down to progressive reductions in net interest margins following the narrowing of spreads between average lending and borrowing rates.

Table 3.4 provides a breakdown of ROA into the single ratios outlined in Sect. 3.3.1 in order to illustrate lenders' strengths and weaknesses and identify trend features.

What is immediately evident from the figures above is that the low level of profitability recorded by German and Italian consumer credit companies in comparison to their Spanish and French counterparts is due principally to higher taxation and, in particular for Italy, lower interest income generated on amounts lent.

The higher tax burden for German and Italian companies means that tax accounts for more than 60%, in Germany, and almost 46%, in Italy, of pre-tax income in comparison to 36% in Spain and 31% in France. The second factor negatively impacting profitability is the lower interest margin recorded by German and Italian consumer credit companies: 3.9% and 3.1% over 4.5% and 5.6% in Spain and France, respectively[32].

As regards year-on-year changes, the drastic reduction in ROA recorded by Italian CCCs in 2006 was the result of a fall in interest margins from 3.81 to 3.07%, higher taxation, which rose from 37 to 46% of pre-tax earnings, and a drop in extraordinary income. These negative changes were only in part offset by a slight

---

[32] As regards Germany, attention should also be drawn to the high level of operating costs which, unlike the other countries in the sample, absorb more than 80% of net interest income. This may in part be due to the limited presence in the country of specialised lenders belonging to banking groups, which typically act as drivers for product and process innovation (see Sect. 3.2.2), increased competition and heightened efficiency.

Table 3.5 Provisions for loan losses (%, 2006)

	2005	2006
France	1.65	1.47
Germany	1.51	1.65
Italy	0.98	1.29
Spain	1.16	1.21

The significance of the differences in average data for the three countries was verified by using the Fischer F-test

improvement in the operating result, which helped to improve the cost/income ratio (the share of operating costs on total operating revenues fell by almost 1%), and increased commission earnings of 30 euro cents for every euro in net interest income in comparison to 20 euro cents in 2005. The increase in non-interest income can be attributed to a broader range of products and services on offer to customers.

The slight improvement in ROA recorded by Spanish consumer credit companies appears to be the result of an increase in interest margins and non-recurring earnings,[33] whilst in France, rises in ROA were due to improved commission earnings, non-recurring items and reduced tax charges.

With regards to the quality of loan portfolios, measured in terms of the provisions for loan losses to total lending ratio (Table 3.5), no statistically significant differences exist between the countries as risk levels in the four markets are substantially similar. However, at year-end 2006 this indicator rose to 1.29% and 1.65% for Italy and Germany, respectively.

3.3.3.1 Profitability and Size

In the next stage, the relation between profitability and size was analysed. On this point, no statistically significant relation between the two variables ($R^2 = 0.0242$ in France, $R^2 = 0.0002$ in Germany, $R^2 = 0.1613$ in Italy, $R^2 = 0.1629$ in Spain,) was seen, as emerges from the high degree of dispersion illustrated in Fig. 3.3.

This result appears to conflict with the theoretical position which states that size allows for cost reduction thanks to the economies of scale generated. However, the absence of a statistically significant relation may stem from the fact that, apart from Germany that has a static market, demand for consumer credit in all the other countries continues to grow (see Sect. 2.2) and some companies have yet to reach the size necessary to exploit economies of scale. Support for this hypothesis is provided by the fact that in all these countries the highest levels of ROA are recorded by the largest companies (Santander in Spain with 4.07%; Cetelem in France with 1.74%; Findomestic in Italy with 1.07%).

---

[33] In general, these positive variations in non-recurring income stemmed from the first time adoption of IAS/IFRS. In Germany, the markedly negative impact non recurring items had on consumer credit lenders' operating results was in line with performances recorded in the banking system as a whole (Bundesbank 2006).

3.3 Profitability Analysis of a Sample of Specialised Consumer Credit Companies 59

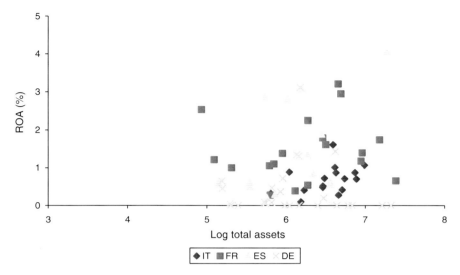

Fig. 3.3 Relation between ROA, total assets and country (2006)

3.3.3.2 Company-Type Analysis

With reference to the company types outlined in Sect. 3.2.1, i.e. specialised finance companies belonging to banking groups and captive companies belonging to manufacturing or retailing groups, in France, Italy and Spain finance companies have higher profitability levels than captives, considerably so in Spain (Table 3.6). This is not the case for Germany, where ROA is higher for captive than for finance companies. This may be due to the composition of the sample and, in particular, to the fact that specialised lenders play a marginal role in a credit market dominated by universal banks.

Differences in profitability levels are mostly due to far lower interest margins earned by captives on their lending and, in Spain and Italy, also the smaller contribution of non-interest income. These performances are directly due to the structural differences that exist between the two company types: captives typically provide funds for the purchase of their parent companies' products as part of a sales strategy that seeks to develop brand loyalty via the conduit of cheaper credit terms.[34] As regards service-generated income, consumer credit companies belonging to banking groups are investing in product portfolios that guarantee a greater role of commission and fee-based revenues in overall net profit.

---

[34] In the Italian market, for instance, Assofin (2007) reports that in the area of motor finance the offer of lower than market rates played an important part in car manufacturers' sales campaigns.

Table 3.6 A breakdown of the ROA by company type (%, 2006)[36]

	ROA	NP/BT	BT/OP	OP/TR	TR/NI	NI/TA
FRANCE						
Finance companies	1.39	72.11	99.73	27.00	124.86	6.30
Captives	1.34	66.13	116.08	26.34	125.18	4.57
GERMANY						
Finance companies	0.36	50.09	41.37	12.84	162.63	3.88
Captives	0.48	22.13	36.01	25.60	191.75	4.05
ITALY						
Finance companies	0.69	54.25	104.69	28.65	137.17	3.21
Captives	0.48	53.87	112.27	31.21	105.72	2.53
SPAIN						
Finance companies	1.56	66.23	122.56	32.00	129.63	5.16
Captives	0.86	61.26	88.42	32.38	116.47	3.55

NP Net profit; *BT* Profit before tax; *OP* Operating profit; *TR* Total operating revenues; *NI* Net interest income; *TA* Total assets

3.3.3.3 Country of Origin Analysis

Finally, differences in ROA on the basis of the country of origin of the consumer credit providers' parent company are shown in Table 3.7. A breakdown of ROA into the five ratios used was not possible for France as the market is prevalently made up by national intermediaries.[35]

For Italy and Spain the results above show higher returns on assets by national CCCs in comparison to those achieved by foreign-owned companies, whilst the opposite is the case in Germany, where ROA recorded by foreign operators, albeit low, are still three times higher than those achieved by domestic lenders. This fact can be put down to the higher levels of net interest and service-generated income typically earned in this case by large-size captives enjoying consolidated positions both at home and abroad (i.e. Toyota Kreditbank GmbH, GMAC Bank GmbH, GE Money Bank GmbH).

3.3.3.4 Multivariate Analysis

The relationship between the overall profitability of consumer credit companies, measured in terms of ROA, and the variables that may explain differences in performance levels was analysed further in order to disentangle the joint effect

---

[35] French companies such as Cetelem (BNP Paribas) and Sofinco (Crédit Agricole) are also particularly aggressive in expanding their international operations.

[36] The significance of differences found amongst average figures cannot be tested owing to the limited number of data resulting from the breakdown of the sample into the two sub-groups – finance companies and captives.

3.3 Profitability Analysis of a Sample of Specialised Consumer Credit Companies 61

Table 3.7 A breakdown of the ROA by country of origin (%, 2006)[37]

	ROA	NP/BT	BT/OP	OP/TR	TR/NI	NI/TA
GERMANY						
Foreign	0.68	32.23	41.33	16.30	179.60	4.26
National	0.20	42.29	37.19	20.15	172.19	3.72
ITALY						
Foreign	0.53	48.18	100.01	29.32	120.87	3.17
National	0.69	56.93	109.18	29.13	135.02	3.02
SPAIN						
Foreign	1.02	62.46	95.62	27.48	124.26	4.67
National	1.77	67.58	134.04	42.46	123.03	3.99

NP Net profit; *BT* Profit before tax; *OP* Operating profit; *TR* Total operating revenues; *NI* Net interest income; *TA* Total assets

these variables may have. A linear regression model with the following equation was used:

$$y_{it} = \alpha_i + \beta_1 x_{it1} + \beta_2 x_{it2} + \ldots + \beta_k x_{itk} + \varepsilon_{it}$$

where y_{it} are the dependent variable observations (ROA) for each consumer credit provider *i* at time *t*, x_{it} is a vector of *k* independent variables for each consumer credit provider *i* at time *t*, β is a vector of parameters of the *k* independent variables whose sign and statistical significativity highlight the possible existence of a relation between ROA and the independent variables, and ε_{it} is the error.

The dataset has a panel structure with cross-section observation n = 75 and time series observation T = 2 (years 2005–2006).

The regressors were chosen to capture the principal features explaining lenders' profitability, i.e. cost structure, profitability of lending activity, diversification and size. Three dummy variables were also included in the equation to take into account two specific characteristics emerging from the descriptive analysis. The first two dummies, *Germany* and *Italy*, are expected to capture, amongst the determinants of ROA, the possible existence of country-specific contextual factors that may play an important role in determining the significant differences between the ROA of the German and the Italian sample and that of the other two countries; the third, *company type*, should capture the differences in profitability existing between finance companies and captives.

The characteristics of the variables are shown in Table 3.8.

Both static panel-data models ("fixed effect" and "random effect") are estimated and results are presented in Appendix (Tables 3.12 and 3.13). The main result is that cost structure and operating presence in Germany and Italy all have a negative impact on ROA. The fixed effect model is supported by the Hausman test.

---
[37] Here again, the significance of differences found amongst average figures cannot be tested owing to the limited number of data resulting from the breakdown of the sample into the two sub-groups – foreign and national.

Table 3.8 Characteristics of dependent variable and regressors

Variable	Description	Expected sign
Dependent variable		
ROA	ROA: Net profit/Total assets	
Independent variables		
SIZE	SIZE: Log total assets	Positive
COST	COST: Cost income ratio	Negative
DIV	DIV: Total operating revenues/net interest income	Positive
MIN	MIN: Net interest income/total assets	Positive
d_I	d_I: *dummy* for Italy	Negative
d_G	d_G: *dummy* for Germany	Negative
d_type	d_type: *dummy* for consumer credit companies belonging to banking groups	Positive

Table 3.9 Weighted leasted squared (WLS) estimations (dependent variable: ROA)

	Coefficient	T-stat
Intercept	0.4320	0.834
d_I	−0.3880***	−3.996
d_G	−0.5977***	−5.960
d_type	0.0881	1.060
SIZE	0.1382*	1.834
COST	−0.0145***	−7.361
DIV	0.0017***	4.137
MIN	8.0944***	5.114

Number of observations: 150
R^2: 0.6280
R^2 correct: 0.6097
F: 34.252 (p-value < 0.00001)

The symbols *, ** and *** indicate significance of, respectively, 10%, 5% and 1%

Clearly, generalisations on the basis of these results should be handled cautiously owing to the very short timeframe of the dataset. In this way the asymptotic results for these models cannot be invoked and, thus, it is not appropriate to perform statistical inference on the parameters. Consequently, the proposed models can only be used to provide a descriptive analysis with the available data.

The final model proposed is the *Weighted Leasted Squared* (WLS)[38]; the coefficient estimates are presented in Table 3.9.

The goodness of fit of the model is measured by R^2 and F test. In the first case, the proportion of the total variation in the dependent variable explained by the independent variables is about 63%, while the F test do not reject the null.

---

[38] This choice was grounded on the following two reasons: the 2 year timeframe may be considered unimportant if the analysis were to focus on changes over time; we also assume that the heteroskedasticity arises only from the individual contribution.

3.3 Profitability Analysis of a Sample of Specialised Consumer Credit Companies

The results highlight that cost structure, the contribution of net interest income to total assets, which is a proxy for the profitability of traditional lending activity, and the contribution of total operating revenues to net interest income, which is a proxy for diversification in activities and, therefore of the part commission margins play in overall profitability, are statistically significant and influence profitability according to the expected sign. In particular, with regards to marginal effects, a one per cent increase in costs to be absorbed by operating income leads to a reduction in ROA of 0.01%, whilst the same increase in net interest income as a share of total assets boosts ROA by more than 8%; a 1% increase in operating revenues as a share of total assets raises ROA by 0.002%.

Lender size, measured in terms of total assets, has a positive effect on ROA. This is consistent with the expected sign and stems from the opportunities economies of scale provide to improve the cost/income ratio. The positive effect size has on ROA did not emerge from the descriptive analysis except in the case of the larger CCCs (Sect. 3.3.3.1).

Finally, as regards the three dummies used into the model, *company type*, *Germany* and *Italy*, the first is not significant whereas the second and the third are: operating in Germany and Italy has a negative impact on ROA. This variable was included amongst the regressors to capture the effect different operating contexts may have on performance, i.e. exogenous factors over which a company's management has little control. The fact that the *Germany* and *Italy* dummies are both negative and significant suggests that the profitability of German and Italian consumer credit providers is influenced by variables that reflect the economic and regulatory environment, and also the level of market competition.

As to this last point, in the case of Germany, the low profitability of CCCs may be a direct effect of the limited presence of specialised financial intermediaries belonging to banking groups, which, as we saw in Sect. 3.2.2 are drivers for heightened innovation, competitiveness and efficiency.[39]

As far as Italy, as we saw in Chap. 2, consumer credit growth rates are high though consumer credit volumes expressed either as a share of GDP or disposable income are comparatively low; factors that make the country a relatively immature market. Lower levels of competitiveness may also hold back the development of product innovation, customer segmentation and cross selling, which will have negative repercussions on lenders' operational efficiency and profitability. Furthermore, institutional factors outlined in Chap 1, such as the efficiency of the justice system, the extent of social capital and the existence of informal credit markets may also generate cross-country differences in growth on both the demand and supply sides of the consumer credit market.

Overall, the analysis of profitability levels shows that currently, at least with regards to France and Spain, specialised consumer credit providers outperform the

---

[39] Weill (2004) states that the operating environment (macroeconomic factors and the structure of the banking system) are important determinants of the cost inefficiencies that characterise German CCCs.

banking industry as a whole. Demand potential is still high, which suggests that consumer credit volumes will continue to grow, albeit at differing rates depending on the degree of market maturity. Both factors will have positive effects on the structure of lenders' costs, as economies of scale lock in, and on commission-based earnings, as product diversification and sophistication bear fruit. The Italian market, still comparatively immature and in a phase of rapid growth, will not miss out on these developments.

At the same time, a changing regulatory environment allied to the likelihood of ever-increasing convergence in consumers' financial behaviour will certainly intensify competition, which in turn will lead to narrower interest margins and heightened risk levels. Forecasted reductions in the quality of lending will inevitably track the diffusion of consumer credit probably also in the near- and sub-prime market segments with high-risk borrowers being most likely to find themselves in conditions of over-indebtedness and default.

Appendix

Table 3.10 Composition of the sample (millions of euros, 2006)

Country	Company Name	Type	Country	Total assets year-end 2006
France	Sofinco	Finance	National	24,165,100
France	Cetelem	Finance	National	15,119,700
France	LaSer Cofinoga	Captive	National	9,138,400
France	Diac	Captive	National	8,823,000
France	Cofidis	Finance	National	4,920,900
France	Finaref	Finance	National	4,554,500
France	Franfinance	Finance	National	3,170,600
France	S2P	Captive	National	2,907,400
France	Mediatis	Finance	National	1,891,358
France	Socram	Finance	National	1,882,900
France	Sygma Banque	Finance	National	1,824,200
France	Financo	Finance	National	1,297,500
France	BMW Finance	Captive	Foreign	1,223,592
France	Banque du Groupe Casino	Captive	National	897,400
France	Gmac Banque	Captive	National	699,000
France	FC France	Captive	Foreign	629,000
France	Banque Solfea	Captive	National	616,800
France	CMP Banque	Finance	National	529,400
France	Cofiloisirs	Finance	National	206,038
France	Novacrdit	Finance	National	123,700
France	Camif	Captive	National	85,412
Germany	Volkswagen Bank GmbH	Captive	National	21,022,699
Germany	Santander Consumer Bank AG	Finance	Foreign	16,312,300
Germany	BMW Bank GmbH	Captive	National	6,782,000
Germany	Mercedes-Benz Bank AG	Captive	National	6,022,700
Germany	TeamBank AG	Finance	National	4,378,000
Germany	Toyota Kreditbank Gmbh	Captive	Foreign	4,156,100
Germany	GMAC Bank GmbH	Captive	Foreign	2,972,000
Germany	GE Money Bank GmbH	Captive	Foreign	2,510,700
Germany	MCE Bank GmbH	Captive	Foreign	1,705,600
Germany	Fiat Bank GmbH	Captive	Foreign	1,506,600
Germany	RBS (RD Europe) GmbH	Finance	Foreign	1,458,300
Germany	Hanseatic Bank GmbH & Co.	Finance	Foreign	1,442,100
Germany	CreditPlus Bank AG	Finance	Foreign	1,356,000
Germany	Dresdner-Cetelem Kreditbank GmbH	Finance	Foreign	1,254,500
Germany	Volvo Auto Bank Deutschland GmbH	Captive	Foreign	1,102,300
Germany	VON ESSEN GmbH & Co KG Bankgesellschaft	Finance	Foreign	957,200
Germany	Allgemeine Beamten Kasse Kreditbank AG	Finance	National	903,800

(*continued*)

Table 3.10 (continued)

Country	Company Name	Type	Country	Total assets year-end 2006
Germany	Augsburger Aktienbank AG	Finance	National	844,200
Germany	FFS Bank GmbH	Captive	National	657,100
Germany	Honda Bank GmbH	Captive	Foreign	655,500
Germany	NetBank AG	Finance	National	546,400
Germany	SKG Bank GmbH	Finance	National	532,700
Germany	readybank ag	Finance	National	248,800
Germany	DZB Bank GmbH	Captive	National	199,400
Germany	NordFinanz Bank AG	Finance	National	196,200
Germany	Aktivbank AG	Finance	National	156,800
Germany	Cronbank AG	Finance	National	154,000
Italy	Findomestic Banca	Finance	National	9,750,900
Italy	Fiat auto F.S.	Captive	National	7,697,284
Italy	Agos	Finance	Foreign	7,364,968
Italy	Fiditalia	Finance	Foreign	5,469,600
Italy	Santander Consumer Bank	Finance	Foreign	5,103,100
Italy	UniCredit Clarima Banca	Finance	National	4,592,900
Italy	Consum.it	Finance	National	4,260,506
Italy	Ducato	Finance	National	4,126,700
Italy	Compass	Finance	National	3,919,100
Italy	Linea–Credito al Consumo	Finance	National	3,146,621
Italy	BancApulia	Finance	National	3,047,700
Italy	BMW F.S.	Captive	Foreign	2,912,682
Italy	Neos Banca	Finance	National	2,902,087
Italy	Gmac Italia	Captive	Foreign	1,830,484
Italy	Daimler Chrysler F.S.	Captive	Foreign	1,822,847
Italy	Micos Banca	Finance	National	1,689,100
Italy	Credifarma	Finance	National	1,534,200
Italy	G.E. Capital F.S.	Captive	Foreign	1,506,194
Italy	Carifin Italia	Finance	National	1,094,000
Italy	Consel	Finance	National	631,300
Italy	BBVA Finanzia	Finance	Foreign	282,491
Spain	Santander Consumer Finance	Finance	National	18,727,801
Spain	Banco Espirito Santo	Finance	Foreign	3,758,700
Spain	Citibank	Finance	Foreign	3,581,000
Spain	Banco de Credito Finanzia	Finance	National	3,573,100
Spain	Banco Cetelem	Finance	Foreign	2,790,400
Spain	G.E. Capital Bank	Captive	Foreign	2,407,500
Spain	Financiera El Corte Ingles	Captive	National	2,228,404
Spain	Volkswagen Finance	Captive	Foreign	1,851,000
Spain	Camge	Finance	National	1,584,008
Spain	Carrefour Servicios Financiero	Captive	Foreign	1,051,200
Spain	Gmac Espana	Captive	Foreign	783,484
Spain	Finconsum	Finance	National	726,088
Spain	DaimlerChrysler Services Espana	Captive	Foreign	568,600

(*continued*)

Appendix

Table 3.10 (continued)

Country	Company Name	Type	Country	Total assets year-end 2006
Spain	Cofidis Hispania	Finance	Foreign	536,200
Spain	Banco Finantia Sofinloc	Finance	Foreign	348,800
Spain	VFS Financial Services Spain	Captive	Foreign	346,500
Spain	Scania Finance	Captive	Foreign	138,824

Table 3.11 Results of the one-way Anova to test for differences among the four countries: F test and significance

	2005	2006
ROA	5.7056***	6.0826**
	(0.0015)	(0.0009)
Net profit/pre-tax profit	2.5664*	7.3624***
	(0.0613)	(0.0002)
Pre-tax profit/Operating profit	7.0702***	6.3130***
	(0.0003)	(0.0007)
Operating profit/total operating revenues	0.8648	1.9965
	(0.4635)	(0.1217)
Total operating revenues/net interest income	2.0455	3.3546**
	(0.1152)	(0.0233)
Net interest income/total assets	2.0306	3.1218**
	(0.1173)	(0.0309)
Provisions for loan losses/total loans	1.2385	0.4180
	(0.3022)	(0.7456)

N.B: the level of Significance of each F test is given in brackets
The symbols *, ** and *** indicate significance of, respectively, 10%, 5% and 1%

Table 3.12 Estimation of fixed effects (dependent variable: ROA)

	Coefficient	T-stat
Intercept		
d_l	−2.0455**	−2.001
d_g	−2.1286**	−2.029
d_type	0.4020	1.647
SIZE	−0.0408	−0.229
COST	−0.0221***	−3.930
DIV	0.0022*	1.822
MIN	6.2269*	1.689

Number of observations: 150
R^2: 0.6154
R^2 correct: 0.1573
F: 1.343 (p-value = 0.105)
The symbols *, ** and *** indicate significance of, respectively, 10%, 5% and 1%

Table 3.13 Estimation of random effects (dependent variable: ROA)

	Coefficient	T-stat
Intercept	1.4295*	1.853
d_l	−0.4290**	−2.502
d_g	−0.7275***	−4.910
d_type	0.0783	0.600
SIZE	0.0318	0.284
COST	−0.0179***	−5.273
DIV	0.0018**	2.240
MIN	n6.7849***	2.957

Number of observations: 150
Variance 'within' = 0.7001
Variance 'between' = 0.1907
Hausman Test: statistic $(x_7^2) = 2.453$, p-value = 0.87

The symbols *, ** and *** indicate significance of, respectively, 10%, 5% and 1%

Chapter 4
From Indebtedness to Over-Indebtedness

4.1 Introduction

The analysis carried out in the previous chapters has highlighted that borrowing certainly gives individuals the possibility of improving lifestyles by smoothing consumption over their life time. However, there are also concerns that some individuals risk a level of indebtedness that is unsustainable in relation to their earnings and that such a situation may lead to over-indebtedness.

In this chapter, we will attempt to provide a definition of over-indebtedness, analysing, in particular, the problems faced in measuring the phenomenon and its determinants. We then look in detail at the measures adopted so far in Europe to prevent ex ante and manage ex post over-indebtedness. The strengths and weaknesses of these measures are analysed in order, where possible, to evaluate the rationale and effectiveness of, at times, widely differing instruments and actions.

4.2 Over-Indebtedness: Defining Features

The complexity of over-indebtedness makes it difficult to define the phenomenon in a clear-cut way.

Generally speaking, over-indebtedness occurs when an individual's level of debt cannot be sustained in relation to current earnings and any additional resources raised from the sale of real or financial assets.[1]

---

[1] This definition is substantially in line with that provided by the European Commission's Group of Specialists for Legal Solutions: "*Over-indebtedness means, but is not limited to, the situation where the debt burden of an individual or a family manifestly and/or on a long-term basis exceeds the payment capacity*" (Group of Specialists for Legal Solutions to Debt Problems CJ-S-DEBT). According to a definition that emphasises the subjective implications of over-indebtedness "*a person is over-indebted if he or she considers that he or she has difficulties in repaying debts, whether consumer debt or a mortgage*" (OCR Macro 2001). Institutional/legal aspects of over-indebtedness have also been defined as part of procedures designed to manage ex post default. These definitions reflect the objectives default management procedures seek to achieve.

This view of over-indebtedness, though substantially capturing the nature of the phenomenon, does not take account of two significant aspects:

- Measurement of the degree of an individual's over-indebtedness
- Identification of the types of over-indebtedness

As regards the first point, the complexity of measuring over-indebtedness stems from, on one hand, the need to establish which liabilities are to be included in the analysis and, on the other, the difficulties arising in determining the threshold beyond which debt levels become excessive. In relation to which liabilities are to be included, above all at the design stage of a debt restructuring programme, in addition to amounts owed to institutional lenders, other commitments should also be taken into account, such as housing costs, taxes and utilities.[2]

On the question of indebtedness types, France's Central bank usefully refers to "active over-indebtedness" and "passive over-indebtedness" (Banque de France 1996). The first is caused by excess debt on the part of an individual due to extensive use of credit in the belief of improved future economic and financial conditions; the second is due to the existence of exogenous factors over which the individual has no control. These factors negatively impact repayment capacity and make what was once a manageable liability no longer sustainable.

Clearly, the distinction between active and passive over-indebtedness is not always easy to make: firstly, because by definition flows of future financial receipts are difficult to forecast and, secondly, by the fact that the two situations are often interrelated, such as in the case of indebted households which, in the face of only a minimum external shock, find it difficult to keep up with debt repayments.

Nevertheless, on a conceptual basis it is important to keep these two types of over-indebtedness distinct. In fact, as will be seen in sect. 4.3, the effectiveness of measures designed to prevent or manage situations of financial difficulty are cause-dependant.

For instance, in Belgium, Law no. 57 of 5th June 1998 relating to the *Reglement collectif de dettes* states that an applicant for debt settlement shall be an individual who "*n'est pas en état, de manière durable, de payer ses dettes exigibles ou encore à échoir*". In France, article 331–1 of the *Code de la Consommation* establishes that "*Le surendettement est la situation dans laquelle se trouvent des personnes physiques don't la situation est caractérisée par l'impossibilité manifeste pour le débiteur de bonne foi de faire face à l'ensemble de ses dettes non professionnelles exigibles et à échoir*". In Germany section 19 of the *Insolvency Statute* of January 2000 provides that "*Over-indebtedness shall exist if the assets owned by the debtor no longer cover his existing obligations to pay*". At present in Italy, no official definition of over-indebtedness exists. Proposed legislation presented in 2006 (no. 412 of 3rd May 2006) defines an individual in a condition of over-indebtedness as one who finds him or herself "*in situation in which on a non-temporary basis there are difficulties in repaying debt commitments on the basis of current earnings and personal assets*".

[2]Financially, an individual is in debt when he/she has loan commitments. However, when an individual is in financial difficulties, he/she will also have problems in respecting other obligations, such as utilities and will, consequently, be indebted also to these service providers.

4.2 Over-Indebtedness: Defining Features

4.2.1 Measuring Over-Indebtedness

Data and indicators generally used for quantifying or identifying situations of financial difficulty can be classified into two groups:[3]

– Aggregate measures
– Individual measures

Each group has a specific informational objective: aggregate measures provide indications regarding the diffusion of financial difficulties in a specific geographic area, whilst individual aggregates provide information about the socio-demographic and economic profiles of individuals and households in financial difficulties (Fig. 4.1).

Aggregate economic data are usually collected by National Central Banks which, referring only to financial liabilities, provide indications as to the level of household indebtedness, the share of current earnings destined to cover debt obligations and the extent of situations of financial difficulties.

In the first case, the most commonly used indicator is the total debt to disposable income ratio. The debt servicing to disposable income ratio measures the share of earnings required to cover debt repayment commitments (principal and interest charges) over a specific period of time.[4]

As regards more specific information concerning situations of financial difficulty, central banks generally collect data referring to late payment, default or any debt cancellations agreed on by the financial system.[5]

In countries equipped with legislation on personal insolvency or debt settlement procedures (see Sect. 4.3.7), aggregate data are also available about individuals who have made use of these procedures. This information, however, underestimates the size of the phenomenon as it refers only to the most serious cases of over-indebtedness, i.e. those that have led to administrative or legal solutions.

Unlike aggregate measures, individual data enables the reconstruction of socio-demographic and economic profiles of individuals experiencing situations of financial difficulties. Such data provide useful insights into the most frequent

---

[3] An analysis is given here of the data and information used to quantify over-indebtedness. For an in-depth discussion of measures tackling over-indebtedness, see a recent work by the European Commission, DG *Employment, Social Affairs and Equal Opportunities* (OEE, CESP, CRPF 2007), which provides a detailed analysis of the principal indicators used to measure over-indebtedness and their availability in the nineteen EU Member States making up the survey.

[4] Clearly, in neither cases can the indicators on their own provide information about individuals' over-indebtedness unless that is each indicator is assigned a threshold beyond which the financial situation is considered unsustainable. The debt/income ratio is recorded in all European countries, whilst the debt servicing to income ratio is, currently, available only in France, Germany, Italy, Lithuania, Poland, Portugal, the United Kingdom and Spain.

[5] For example, the Bank of France, in its *Fichier des incidents de remboursement des* crédits *aux particuliers* (FICP) provides details of the total amount owed by households for arrears corresponding to at least two instalments or 60 days, whilst the Bank of Greece reports on an annual basis late payments in mortgage and consumer credit instalments. The Bank of Italy also gives details of payment arrears amongst households in its regular statistical bulletins.

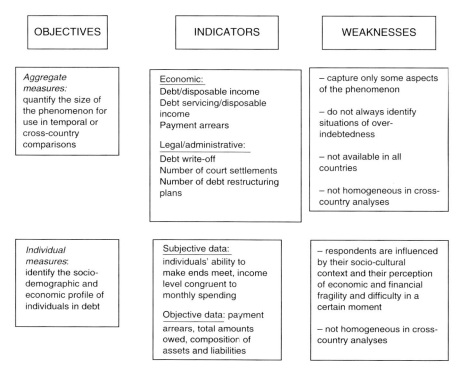

Fig. 4.1 Indicators of over-indebtedness

causes of over-indebtedness and play an important role in the design of measures for the prevention and management of the phenomenon.

These data are generally collected via surveys, organised by Central Banks or national statistics institutes, which contain questions referring both to respondents' perceptions of the congruity of their earnings in relation to spending and their ability to make ends meet as well as questions that ask individuals to provide details of indebtedness levels, debt servicing, payment arrears, income and the composition of assets and liabilities.[6]

---

[6]In Europe, national panel surveys are organised and published in only five countries: Austria (*Survey on Financial Assets of Private households*); Italy (*Survey of Households Income and Wealth* – SHIW); Luxembourg (*Socio-economic Panel Life*), United Kingdom (*British Households Panel Survey* – BHPS); Spain (*Survey of Household Finances* – EFF). At European level, information in part regarding individuals' financial conditions is collected by Eurobarometer and by EU-SILC. Nevertheless, neither currently collects information relating specifically to situations of individual over-indebtedness (this formation will be collected by EU-SILC starting from 2008 survey). Furthermore, limits in size (Eurobarometer) and timespan (EU-SILC) mean that data generated by either survey is of limited use for detailed analyses.

It should be pointed out that both aggregate and individual measures must be used with care when performing cross-country analyses as these investigations run up against difficulties in achieving homogeneousness in, for instance, the definition of solvency, late payment and income (real, nominal, equivalent) in addition to differences in the frequency of surveys and the characteristics of respondents.

4.2.2 Possible Causes of Over-Indebtedness

Various studies into financial difficulties amongst households, both from an economic and behavioural perspective, have focused on the reasons for over-indebtedness. Such studies are typically based on quantitative empirical research carried out by central banks or statistics institutes as well as on interview-based surveys of households in financial difficulty.

With regards to economic analyses, an important and regularly cited cause of over-indebtedness is low income levels that make it difficult to repay a debt (Del Rio and Young 2005a; Bridges and Disney 2004; Rinaldi and Sanchez-Arellano 2006; Kempson 2002; OEE 2005; Korczak 2000).[7]

In the behavioural economics literature, over-indebtedness is frequently seen as the result of individuals' actions, such as: inability to manage household finances effectively and make consumption choices on the basis of available resources; spending and life-style habits that cannot be sustained by disposable financial and economic resources and which are therefore financed by debt (Waldron and Young 2006; Costa and Pinto 2005; Rowlingson and Kempson 1993; Elliott 2005; Frade 2004; DTI-MORI 2005; OEE 2005; Gloukoviezoff 2006; Koljonen and Romer-Paakkanen 2000; Haas 2006; Farinha 2004; Johansson and Persson 2006; Mori 2003; Kish 2006; Vandone and Anderloni 2008).

Such behaviour can often be put down to social and psychological factors that reduce an individual's capacity to evaluate the consequences of his/her consumption and borrowing decisions, which may not be rational from an economic point of view.[8] Individuals in fact tend, on one hand, to overestimate their capacity to

---

[7]Studies in the United Kingdom show that 15% of households suffering financial difficulties are in this condition as a result of low incomes (Kempson 2002). In Belgium 19% of individuals seeking insolvency provisions for the cancellation of their debt blamed low incomes for their present condition (OEE 2005); similar findings come from research carried out in Germany (Korczak 2000, Reifner et al. 2007). It should be pointed out that such data are not directly comparable owing to differences in life styles and attitudes to consumption and indebtedness. Furthermore, the sample of individuals taking part in the survey often differ, i.e. in some cases respondents are individuals having applied for debt settlement, whilst others are interviewees taken from the population at large.

[8]A analysis of the psychological aspects that influence individuals' savings and consumption decisions is provided in Chap. 1 (Sect. 1.4) along with a discussion of behavioural phenomena such as "excess optimism", "availability heuristic" and the "hyperbolic discounting factor". See also Poppe (2008) who argues that "an adequate understanding of the debt problem phenomenon presupposes a social rather than an economic perspective and that any set of remedial steps to

manage domestic financial resources and, on the other, to underestimate the possibility of being affected by negative events, such as illness or job loss.

As a result, these individuals systematically underestimate the risk of not being able to meet their financial commitments (Kilborn 2005; Meier and Sprenger 2007). Furthermore, they overestimate the immediate benefits and undervalue the future costs; such behaviour leads to the decision to purchase, using debt if necessary, regardless of the effect this choice may have on the sustainability of future debt levels (Meier and Sprenger 2007).

Numerous studies suggest that over-indebtedness is also due to institutional factors, such as the efficiency of the legal system or the efficiency of information-sharing mechanisms in place amongst lenders, which influence above all an individual's willingness to repay a debt rather than his or her capacity to do so. As far as the efficiency of the legal system, a question covered in detail in Chap. 1 (Sect. 1.2.1), the likelihood of repayment delays or insolvency increases when legal costs and repossession or foreclosure times rise as such inefficiencies increase opportunistic behaviour on the part of borrowers (Duygan and Grant 2008). The absence of information-sharing mechanisms also increases incentives to apply for loans at more than one institution because the household's debt exposure to the system is substantially unknown (Jappelli and Pagano 2006).

What emerges from much research is that over-indebtedness is in many cases "passive", i.e. due to a reduction in income following an unexpected or adverse event. Such an event, which negatively impacts an individual's financial situation, is principally the result of a change in employment conditions, for instance job loss, or a reduction in working hours, a change in the composition of the household, such as the birth of a child or separation, death, illness or injury (Koljonen and Romer-Paakkanen 2000; Gloukoviezoff 2006; Kempson 2002).[9]

On the basis of the findings so far discussed, it is possible to identify the type of over-indebtedness – "active" and "passive" – on the basis of the causes that determine it (Fig. 4.2).

In the first case, over-indebtedness is generated by excessive levels of debt held by households, following decisions to borrow up to a level that is unsustainable on the basis of present or future earnings. Such decisions may be due to:

---

[9]In France, 72% of individuals in a condition of over-indebtedness find themselves in this situation as a result of an unexpected event that led to a fall in available income (Banque de France 2005), whilst in the United Kingdom, the same cause accounts for 50% of cases (Kempson 2002). Staying in France, job loss (34.6%) represents the primary cause of over-indebtedness due to a fall in earnings, with divorce in second place, accounting for 14.7% (Banque de France 2005, Le Duigou 2000). In Germany, also, Reifner et al. (2007) show that divorce and separation represent the second cause for over-indebtedness after job loss. In the United Kingdom, however, Waldron and Young (2006) and DTI-MORI (2005) reveal that divorce is a less common cause of financial difficulty; results for Portugal show that divorce comes after illness, low earnings and unemployment as cause for over-indebtedness (Observatorio do endividamento 2002). In Finland, the loss of a job also emerges as a significant reason for over-indebtedness, above all amongst younger age groups (Koljonen and Romer-Paakkanen 2000).

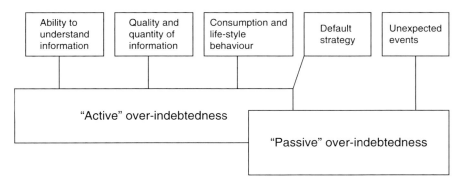

Fig. 4.2 The causes of over-indebtedness

- Individuals' inability to process effectively information available and, as a result, to evaluate the consequences of indebtedness
- Lack of information transparency that hinders well-informed decision-making
- Consumption and life-style behaviours which, either due to irresponsibility or short-sightedness, lead an individual to non optimal consumption and indebtedness choices
- Borrowing choices made knowing that amounts owed will not be repaid (strategic default)

In the second case, i.e. passive over-indebtedness, financial difficulties are determined by unexpected factors beyond an individual's control, such as job loss, separation, death or illness, changes in macroeconomic variables (i.e. interest rate hikes) or higher taxation. These factors can eliminate or reduce an income source and/or determine unexpected liabilities.

It is reasonable to believe that over-indebtedness is more often than not the result of a combination of causes arising either from excessive levels of individual debt or unexpected events that make the debt contracted no longer sustainable. The problem clearly requires to be addressed on several fronts in order to identify which policies should be adopted to prevent the phenomenon and contain ex post its effects.

4.3 Policy Measures for the Prevention and Management of Over-Indebtedness

Measures designed to address the phenomenon of over-indebtedness are usually categorised into those that seek ex ante preventive solutions and those aimed at providing assistance to individuals and households already in financial difficulty.

Preventive measures recognise the critical importance of behaviour patterns in determining situations of financial difficulty. They can be classified into:

- "Responsible borrowing" measures
- "Responsible lending" measures

Both sets of measures have dual aims: on one hand, to avoid active over-indebtedness; on the other, to prevent or reduce the seriousness of passive over-indebtedness by offering advice and solutions that allow households to manage more effectively the effects of adverse shocks that can negatively impact their financial situation.

Responsible borrowing measures mainly consist of financial education and debt counselling services designed to raise awareness about the implications of debt and to help individuals fix levels of debt that do not lead to financial difficulties. Penalties for late or non payment if made clear before entering the credit market can also act as an effective deterrent for strategic insolvency.

Responsible lending includes a raft of measures such as: mandatory disclosure and transparency requirements on the part of financial intermediaries regarding the terms and conditions of loans; appropriate scoring procedures of the applicant's creditworthiness and total level of exposure; flexible approach to early warning signs of indebted households in difficulty; the fixing within certain limits of interest rate ceilings on lending to customers.

Ex post debt management schemes in the form of debt settlement procedures aim to provide individuals in difficulty with the possibility of restructuring their debts and in some cases the cancellation of parts of it.

Table 4.1 summarises the causes of over-indebtedness discussed in Sect. 4.2 along with possible measures for its prevention and management, while the following paragraphs will focus on how and to what extent these measures prevent, contain or combat over-indebtedness.

We wish, however, to underline that any evaluation of the effectiveness of these measures should necessarily take into account the following three points:

1. No policy designed to prevent or manage over-indebtedness can on its own solve the problem. The composite nature of the phenomenon requires adopting strategies that provide solutions equipped concurrently to prevent ex ante unsustainable levels of indebtedness and to support ex post individuals and households in the restructuring of their debt.
2. Preventive measures alone cannot guarantee optimal responsible borrowing and lending. For this reason, it is essential to design ex post solutions for insolvent individuals and households that through restructuring and debt settlement give the opportunity of a fresh start.
3. Responsible lending measures can help financial intermediaries evaluate correctly borrowers' exposures and provide applicants for a loan with all the information they need to make a responsible borrowing decision. However, we do not support possible legislative solutions that propose assigning responsibility for individuals' over-indebtedness to financial intermediaries. Such a move is unrealistic as financial intermediaries, by nature, evaluate the impact that a loan may have on their balance sheets, but do not consider possible negative externalities generated from the granting of a loan on households' well-being.[10]

---

[10]For an analysis of the problems raised by assigning responsibility for individuals' over-indebtedness to financial intermediaries, see Anderloni (1997) and Filotto and Nicolini (2007), Reifner et al. (2003).

4.3 Policy Measures for the Prevention and Management of Over-Indebtedness 77

Table 4.1 Relations between possible causes of over-indebtedness and measures for its prevention and management

Determinants	Preventive measures			
	Responsible borrowing		Responsible lending	
	Instrument	Objective	Instrument	Objective
Excess debt ("Active" over-indebtedness)				
Inability to understand information	Financial education	To improve individuals' capabilities in understanding information available so as to evaluate the sustainability of borrowing decisions	Credit bureaus	The use of positive information supplied by credit bureaus allows lenders to have a more complete picture of an individual's total debt exposure. This information may lead to a rejected application for credit if the individual is not able to understand correctly the information available and therefore is not in a position to assess the sustainability of the debt requested
	Debt counselling	To provide individuals with advice concerning the management of household finances and decisions regarding consumption, savings and borrowing	Interest rate ceilings	With ceilings in place, financial intermediaries do not lend to high-risk customers because if they did, the rate applied would be higher than the maximum amount established by law
Limited transparency of information	Transparency and completeness of information	To give individuals the essential informational tools necessary for an informed and responsible borrowing decision	Transparency and completeness of information	Mandatory market disclosure requirements entail the provision on the part of financial intermediaries of complete and correct information

(*continued*)

Table 4.1 (continued)

Determinants	Preventive measures			
	Responsible borrowing		Responsible lending	
	Instrument	Objective	Instrument	Objective
Non rational consumption choices	Financial education	To create greater awareness on the part of individuals of the financial consequences of their spending decisions	Credit bureaus	Also in this case, positive information supplied by credit bureaus allows intermediaries to have a more informed picture of an individual's overall debt exposure, thereby avoiding over-indebtedness due to an inability to evaluate the consequences of spending, savings and indebtedness choices
	Debt counselling	To improve the capability of individuals to evaluate the consequences of consumption and life-style habits by raising knowledge levels regarding the management of household finances	Interest rate ceilings	With ceilings in place, financial intermediaries do not lend to high-risk customers because if they did, the rate applied would be higher than the maximum amount established by law
	Penalties for late payment	To use clear and transparent information regarding the penalties that will be incurred for late payment so as to reduce the influence of psychological factors, such as hyperbolic discount and availability heuristic, which tend to induce individuals to underestimate the consequences of their actions		

(continued)

4.3 Policy Measures for the Prevention and Management of Over-Indebtedness 79

Table 4.1 (continued)

Determinants	Preventive measures			
	Responsible borrowing		Responsible lending	
	Instrument	Objective	Instrument	Objective
Strategic default	Credit bureaus	To deter individuals from strategically defaulting by making them aware of the negative consequences such behaviour will have on future applications for credit	Credit bureaus	The negative information supplied by credit bureaus allows intermediaries to have a more informed picture of an individual's repayment behaviour, thereby reducing the risk of granting credit to delinquent borrowers
	Penalties for late payment	To deter individuals from strategically defaulting by making them aware of the penalties they will incur during debt settlement procedures		
Unexpected events ("Passive" over-indebtedness)				
Unexpected events such as job loss, divorce or separation, negative changes in interest rates, cost of living, taxes	Financial education	To improve individuals' capabilities in understanding and using instruments designed to reduce the impact of unexpected events	Arrears management	Flexible and prompt arrears management solutions applied at the early warning stage of temporary indebtedness can increase the likelihood that a loan returns to a performing status rather than degenerating into insolvency
	Debt counselling	To help individuals choose the right instruments to address the effects of unexpected events by planning and managing household finances more effectively		

4.3.1 Financial Education

Amongst preventive measures that seek to achieve more responsible borrowing by individuals, financial education plays an important role, by addressing three causes in particular of over-indebtedness.[11]

Firstly, financial education seeks to improve individuals' capacity to understand financial information, raise awareness about the risks and consequences of their borrowing decisions and to help them choose the right financial products for their needs.[12]

Secondly, financial education targets behaviour patterns due to inability, irresponsibility or short-sightedness that lead individuals into excess debt. By helping individuals understand the difference between what they want and what they need and between essential items and those that can be purchased at a later date, significant inroads into the behavioural causes of over-indebtedness can be made.

Thirdly, financial education sets out to limit the negative impact that unexpected events can have on household finances. Increased financial knowledge in fact helps individuals to manage more effectively their finances and put into place, for instance, savings or insurance solutions designed to safeguard their financial future.[13]

Within the European Union, financial education is viewed as a key factor in helping individuals make informed choices regarding savings or borrowing.[14] On this point, the European Commission has recently adopted a Communication on Financial Education,[15] which stresses the importance of increasing the ability of Europe's citizens to understand and use financial products and services since increased financial literacy can "... assist adults in planning for major events like buying a home or becoming parents. It can help citizens make better financial provision for unforeseen situations, invest wisely and save for their retirement.

---

[11] For details regarding the objectives, instruments, users and providers of financial education see amongst many others FSA (2005), FSA (2006), Molyneux (2006), Anderloni et al. (2006), GAO (2006). Financial education is a multi-faceted question which, however, for the purposes of this paper is analysed exclusively in relation to the problem of over-indebtedness. The principal instruments of promoting financial literacy by means of financial education include teaching programmes for school children and adults, government campaigns through the mass media, consumer associations, banking associations, web-based initiatives, interactive games as well as what is learned from other individuals.

[12] We should however be wary of the risk of viewing financial education as a convenient panacea. Indeed, the model that posits the sequence "*financial education $\rightarrow$ financial literacy $\rightarrow$ good financial decision and behaviour*" may be flawed. For an interesting recent critique of financial education, see Willis (2008a), Tatom and Godsted (2006) and Hathaway and Khatiwada (2008).

[13] Payment Protection Insurance: see Chap. 3, Sect. 3.2.2.

[14] The question of financial education is the subject of wider debate outside the European Union, in particular in the United States, Canada and Australia. See OECD (2005), Consumer and Financial Literacy Task Force (2004), AC Nielsen – Anz (2005), World Bank (2005).

[15] European Commission Communication on Financial Education, 18th December 2007.

4.3 Policy Measures for the Prevention and Management of Over-Indebtedness

It can help people to avoid the pitfalls of payment fraud. People who understand financial issues make better choices of financial services for their particular needs and are more inclined to heed regulatory risk warning. They are less likely to purchase products they do not need, be tied into products that they do not understand, or take risks that could drive them into financial difficulties". Measures adopted to implement financial education differ from Member State to Member State[16] in terms of end users (young people and adults), organising bodies (government, industry, schools,[17] non profit organisations) and content (general or specific topics, such as over-indebtedness).

In Europe, the United Kingdom appears to have the most extensive measures relating to the question of financial education (FSA 2005, 2006). The Financial Services Authority, in collaboration with the UK Government, has in fact implemented the National Financial Capability Strategy, which foresees financial education solutions targeted at different segments of the population, such as school children, young adults, adults, first-time parents and employees. As regards instruments specifically designed to prevent over-indebtedness, this programme includes an on line Financial Healthcheck that offers "tips for a healthier financial lifestyle – now and in the future".[18] In 2005, the FSA also set up the Financial Capability Innovation Fund with the aim of funding financial literacy projects offered by non profit organisations.

Also in Sweden, financial education is managed centrally by an independent agency, the Swedish Consumers' Banking and Finance Bureau, whose board of directors includes representatives from the Swedish Financial Authority and banking and consumer associations. Amongst the agency's core purposes is the processing and provision for consumers of information relating to financial services and products and their costs so as help individuals make informed savings and borrowing decisions.

In Germany, financial education initiatives are presently organised on a voluntary basis and consist mainly in support offered by debt counselling agencies or consumer associations.

---

[16]In its Communication of 18th December 2007, the European Commission stresses the fact that financial education initiatives should be taken directly by individual Member States as they are in a better position to identify the measures to be implemented and the population segments to be targeted. As in other policy areas, the EU has an overarching role to provide support and raise awareness. An example of EU initiatives in the area of financial education includes Dolceta (Development of On Line Consumer Education Tools for Adults), which contains sections on consumer credit and steps to be taken in the event of repayment difficulties.

[17]Financial education for young people, which aims also to help prevent certain financial problems in later life, is an integral and compulsory part of national school curricula in Norway and Greece. In most European countries, however, the provision of financial education initiatives comes from outside the school system and on an irregular basis.

[18]The FSA's "Financial Healthcheck" is an on line questionnaire that uses respondents' replies to build up a picture of their overall financial situation both in the short and medium-term and to suggest ways of improving it. www.moneymadeclear.fsa.gov.uk.

In Italy and France, measures for increased financial literacy are principally organised by the countries' banking associations: *Pattichiari* in Italy and *Les mini-guides bancaire* in France.

In Spain too financial education initiatives are not organised on a centralised basis, but in the form of information schemes voluntary provided by various associations. For instance, CEACCU (*Confederacion Espanola de Organizaciones de Amas de Casa, Consumidores Y Usuarios*) offers fact sheets that explain consumer rights and describe in jargon-free language the range of borrowing solutions available in order to help individuals evaluate their level of indebtedness and their exposure to financial difficulties (CEACCU 2007).

With regards to measures designed specifically to prevent over-indebtedness, an important contribution is offered by software packages which, on the basis of an individual's socio-economic and financial details, can provide a summary of his or her financial situation and the impact a particular level of debt would have in addition to its sustainability.

In these models, users insert details necessary for the programme to calculate the effects a loan would have on household finances and provides output that can be used to assess whether the debt is sustainable or not. Unlike financial education schemes, which tend to have effects in the long term, these on-line solutions have the advantage of producing real time support for borrowing decisions. Nevertheless, particular attention has to be paid to acquiring information in the correct way, to process it on the basis also of an individual's particular preferences and to provide information that can be used easily in assessing the sustainability of debt.[19]

Schemes adopted to promote financial literacy should also be periodically monitored for their effectiveness. Two reasons in support of this position come to mind: firstly, as these initiatives receive also public funds it is appropriate that the results of such investments are assessed; secondly, some individuals on the basis of the financial education received may overrate their ability to evaluate correctly the risk and subsequent impact, for instance, of taking out a loan.[20]

---

[19]For a detailed analysis of the advantages and difficulties connected to implementing and using on-line solutions, see Filotto and Nicolini (2007). In the United States, private-sector software packages have been available for several years which, though not aiming to evaluate a user's financial situation, provide support in the borrowing decision-making process. Loan Expert Plus, for example, is a programme that calculates the real cost of mortgages and loans and enables users to compare quickly various products. Quicken 2007 Deluxe, on the other hand, is a finance management software package designed to plan households' financial inflows and outflows.

[20]Willis (2008b) makes the telling point that *"turning cognitive literacy into positive action requires a well-calibrated degree of confidence – neither underconfidence nor overconfidence. Consumers' belief about the efficacy of their own financial decision making must match the actual and perceived difficulty of the decision at hand. Overconfident consumers are unlikely to ask for help when they need it and will spend too little time and effort on financial decisions. Underconfident consumers tend to shy away from engaging in the information search, planning, and calculations that good financial decisions require"*.

4.3.2 Debt Counselling Agencies

Debt counselling agencies offer households advice about running their finances. They contribute to the prevention of over-indebtedness both by increasing an individual's ability to understand financial information relating to the state of his or her financial assets and liabilities and by helping raise awareness about the effects consumption and life-style behaviour has on a household's finances.

Debt counselling also offers support to households already in a situation of over-indebtedness in the form of out-of-court agreements, formal debt settlement procedures and, in some cases, finance at special terms.

The range of services offered varies from country to country as does the institutional type, which may be either a government or local government agency, such as in Finland, Sweden and Norway, or bodies belonging to non profit associations, such as Ireland's Money Advice and Budgeting Service (MABS), operating since 1992.[21] In certain cases, these agencies are financed also by banks, which, thanks to agency intervention, pays a percentage on the loans recovered.[22]

In some countries, such as the Netherlands and Austria, persons offering debt counselling have to have specific qualifications that are externally certified, whilst in other countries, such as Belgium and the United Kingdom, counselling agencies and the services they can and cannot offer are subject to authorisation by competent regulatory bodies. In Italy, the consumers' association *Adiconsum* offers consultancy and free psychological support for over-indebted households that apply for financial support from the Usury Prevention Fund.[23]

4.3.3 Credit Bureau

Financial education initiatives and the services provided by debt counselling agencies certainly help to improve individuals' abilities to borrow responsibly. However, these measures on their own cannot be realistically expected to prevent over-indebtedness. Individuals, in fact, may continue to have difficulties understanding correctly the financial information made available to them or may not be able to alter significantly behaviour patterns that lead them to over-borrow.

---

[21]For an overview of services offered by MABS see Korczak (2004). For Finland see Valkama (2004).

[22]This form of support given to debt counselling agencies often represents a form of marketing by a bank in a particular geographic area (Anderloni 1997).

[23]This Fund – *Fondo di Prevenzione Usura* – is provided with financial support by banks and is targeted at over-indebted households. By providing guarantees, the Fund allows banks to grant loans to individuals and households that otherwise would be excluded from the formal credit circuit.

In addition, some individuals will continue to contract credit without any real intention of repaying amounts owed.

With these points in mind, responsible lending measures, which assign lenders a decisive role in avoiding situations of over-indebtedness, are of the utmost importance.

These measures depend above all on financial institutions' having the resources to assess the reason for the loan and the overall financial situation of the prospective borrower.[24] Clearly, the quantity and quality of information the lender can access regarding the applicant's socio-demographic and economic profile, repayment history and overall debt exposure will be vitally important. This information may already be available in an intermediary's own customer records, gleaned directly from the customer or acquired from a credit bureau.

Credit bureaus play an important preventive role for two reasons. Firstly, because they supply information concerning an individual's total level of indebtedness, which puts a lender in a position to decide whether to grant further credit. Secondly, because credit bureaus supply information regarding an individual's repayment track record; on one hand this limits the risk of financial institutions' lending to individuals that have already experienced repayment problems and, on the other, reduces the incentive for individuals to adopt default strategies in the knowledge that payment arrears on loans contracted with one institution will damage their credit reputation system-wide.

The effectiveness of credit bureaus in preventing the risk of over-indebtedness depends also on their specific characteristics and therefore the type of information they can collect, how long they can store it, whether the bureau is a public or private sector body, etc.[25]

On the question of information type, credit bureaus can be divided into those that collect negative or positive information; the former is reputational information that relates exclusively to individuals in arrears or insolvency, whilst the latter is information regarding all borrowers including those in performing situations.

Access by borrowers to records providing details of their own credit history reinforce credit bureaus' credibility and therefore their preventive role against over-indebtedness. Borrowers in this way not only can check the correctness of the information regarding them, but can also use it to improve their credit scores.

Table 4.2 summarises the main benefits and costs of credit bureaus.

The considerable differences in credit bureaus across Europe probably stem from difficulties in assessing and quantifying the trade offs between costs and benefits present in the various information-sharing models that exist. In France, Denmark, Finland and Norway, for example, credit bureaus hold exclusively negative information, whilst in the United Kingdom, Italy, Spain and Sweden bureaus hold both

---

[24]Lenders should be aware primarily of the importance of evaluating the purpose of the loan in order to determine its risk profile and profitability.

[25]See Miller (2005), Chandler and Parker (1989), Jappelli and Pagano (1993) and Vercammen (1995) for details of various types of credit bureaus.

Table 4.2 Credit bureaus: benefits and costs

Benefits	Costs
Reduce active over-indebtedness as lenders have information on individuals' overall debt exposure and repayment history	Increased costs for the credit industry
Reduce the likelihood of strategic default and increase incentives to repay	Problems relating to privacy and personal data handling
Reduce industry entry costs for new players (above all foreign)	Uncertainty of lower prices as some prices are inelastic (i.e. credit cards)
Increase competition between lenders, which generates wider product supply and lower prices	Risk that information collected may not be accurate or complete (the importance of individuals' access to own records)
Make access to credit easier and improve terms and conditions applied	Effectiveness depends on type of information collected and number of years stored
	Information collected relates principally to financial indebtedness
	Information relates to repayment history, but does not take into account unexpected events (passive over-indebtedness)

negative and positive forms of information. Furthermore, in Spain, Norway and the United Kingdom negative information not only provides details of amounts owed to financial institutions, but also of individuals' situations relating to tax and utilities commitments, with the Swedish credit bureau also providing information about individuals' income levels.

Credit institutions' assessment of households' creditworthiness, along with individuals' overall level of indebtedness and the responsible lending such assessments implies, is normally carried out on a voluntary basis, with lenders having an obvious incentive to monitor their customers effectively. However, in some countries laws exist that make assessment mandatory. In Belgium, for instance, the Law of 10th August 2001 relating to the *Centrale des Crédits aux Particuliers* establishes that financial intermediaries shall acquire information regarding the financial situation and solvency of an applicant for credit before approving a loan; non adherence to this regulation will lead to partial or total cancellation of the loan.[26] Further

---

[26]Article 9 of Law 10/8/2001 relating to the *Centrale des Crédits aux Particuliers* states that: "*Afin d'obtenir des informations sur la situation financiére et la solvabilité de l'emprunteur les preteurs consultent la Centrale préalablement à la conclusion d'un contract de crédit à la consommation ou à la remise d'une offre de crédit hypothécaire*". Article 16: "*Sans préjudice des sanctions de droit commun, le juge peut d'office relever l'emprunteur de tout ou partie des intérets de retard et réduire ses obligations jusqu'au prix au comptant du bien ou du service, ou au montant emprunté lorsque le preteur ne s'est pas conformé aux obligations visées à l'article 9*".

legislation designed to encourage effective creditworthiness assessment by lenders of counterpart risk is that relating to the *Règlement collectif de dettes* of 5th June 1998, which provides that every financial intermediary shall make annual provisions to the *Fonds de Traitement du Surendettement* in proportion to the number of bad loans on its books.[27]

As we have already mentioned, responsible lending initiatives that require lenders to evaluate correctly their customers' level of indebtedness and repayment ability are essential. We are not in favour, however, of measures which, by accepting the principle that banks and other financial intermediaries are responsible for their customers' default or insolvency, limit their right to recover amounts owed.

4.3.4 Transparent Information

In order for an individual to make a responsible borrowing decision on the basis of the product description available, the information describing the loan has to be clear, transparent, correct and comprehensive in addition to being expressed in such a way that makes it fully and correctly understandable.

Consequently, financial intermediaries have to provide information – product description, terms and economic conditions applied, measures adopted in the event of payment arrears, terms and conditions relating to variations in instalments – which allow individuals to make a responsible and informed borrowing decision and to compare products easily.[28]

It is essential that such transparency provisions should also apply to instalment payment plans signed directly between retailers and customers: dealers, having strong incentives to sell consumer credit products, on one hand, tend to use aggressive marketing strategies, such as rapid no hassle loans, discounts for consumer credit purchases, etc., and, on the other, are not always able to provide complete and exact information about the loan agreements their customers are signing.

The transparency and completeness of information is generally guaranteed by legal safeguards aimed to protect the consumer both during the promotion of the financial products and at the moment of concluding the contract. In France, for example, the law states that all information offered prior to the conclusion of the contract should be made widely available and be presented in a standardised form so as to make comparison between different lenders' products easier.[29] In the United

---

[27]Article 20, paragraph 2 of the Law relating to the Règlement collectif de dettes of 5th June 1998 states: "*Pour alimenter le Fonds, chaque preteur est tenu de payer une cotisation annuelle, calculée sur la base d'un coefficient appliqué sur le montant total des arriérés de paiment des contrats de crédits qu'il fait enregistrer dans la Centrale des Crédits aux Particuliers gérée par la Banque Nationale de Belgique. . . . Le calcul de la cotisation s'effectue sur la base des défaults de paiment enregistrés au 31 décembre de l'année qui précéde l'année où la cotisation est due....*".

[28]To this end, the annual percentage rate of interest (APR) expresses the total cost of a loan and must be stated in consumer credit contracts (see Chap. 5, Sect. 5.3.2.1).

[29]Loi Scrivenier, 1978 "*Information et protection del consummateurs dans la domaine de certaines operations de credit*".

Kingdom, consumer credit law obliges credit suppliers to provide borrowers with regular updates about outstanding amounts and any arrears.[30] The new Consumer Credit Directive is expected to increase transparency in consumer credit contracts by raising information requirements (see chap. 5).

4.3.5 Responsible Arrears Management

Preventive measures within the category of responsible lending include also arrears management procedures. Flexible and prompt arrears management solutions applied at the early warning stage of temporary financial difficulties can increase the likelihood that a loan returns to a performing status rather than degenerating into insolvency.

Such measures are mainly used on a voluntary basis by utilities companies and include various solutions in the design of repayment schedules (Dominy and Kempson 2003).

In the United Kingdom, OfWat, the water industry watchdog, has established sector-wide guidelines for arrears management that consist in a timely response to early warning signs of payment difficulty along with a range of flexible and sustainable repayment solutions. In the banking industry, however, ex post solutions for the consolidation, restructuring and retiming of non performing loans are generally missing.

4.3.6 Interest Rate Ceilings and Usury Laws

A final form of responsible lending measures aimed at preventing over-indebtedness is the fixing of interest rate ceilings on loans contracted.

As regards lending to households, in theory the fixing of interest rate limits acts in two ways to prevent over-indebtedness: firstly, it prevents granting credit to high-risk individuals and, secondly, it contains borrowing costs for those who have obtained a loan.

The situation in Europe varies both with regards to whether and in what way such limits are fixed: there are countries in which no specific regulations are in place and countries in which interest-rate ceilings are fixed by law, monitored by credit authorities, such as national central banks, with penalties for those applying usury rates.[31]

---

[30]Fair Trading Act, 1973.

[31]For details of existing anti usury laws, see the European Commission DG Employment, Social Affairs and Equal Opportunities (OEE, CESP, CRPF 2007).

The effectiveness of regulatory limits on the cost of borrowing is however far from decisive. When the cost of extending credit is higher than a pre-set limit, financial intermediaries do not lend, with the apparent effect that borrowers most at risk of over-indebtedness and insolvency are excluded from the credit market. However, one obvious result of exclusion from formal credit solutions is to push high-risk individuals into illegal markets where borrowing costs are much higher.

In other words, the fixing of interest-rate ceilings does not stop individuals from borrowing money nor does it reduce the level of debt since above all individuals most at risk of social exclusion and therefore over-indebtedness are those most likely to borrow.[32]

4.3.7 Debt Settlement Procedures

The responsible borrowing and lending measures described in the sections above aim to prevent over-indebtedness. However effective these initiatives may be, they cannot eliminate over-indebtedness completely. This is particularly true in the case of passive over-indebtedness, which, as we have seen, depends much more on the negative impact of unexpected events rather than on an individual's ability to avoid excessive levels of personal debt.

Bearing this in mind, measures, such as debt settlement procedures, which address ex post situations of financial difficulty play a fundamental role not only in helping individuals rebuild their lives, but also in deterring strategic insolvencies and irresponsible borrowing decisions via the sanctions these procedures foresee and the social stigma associated with insolvency in many communities.[33]

---

[32] In the United Kingdom, a report by the Department of Trade and Industry (DTI 2003), subsequently disbanded and replaced by the new Department for Business, Enterprise and Regulatory Reform in June 2007, underlined the importance of not fixing interest-rate ceilings on loans. Also in France, the need has been expressed to review anti-usury measures as lending interest-rate limits were too low in relation to the risks that would be generated from lending to near and subprime borrowers, potential customer segments that are currently excluded from the formal credit market (BITE, 2006). For a detailed analysis of the problems connected to applying interest-rate ceilings see Baudassé and Lavigne (2000), who underlines that the principal difficulties of usury laws lie in defining credit categories and the choice of formula used for calculating usury rates. See also Filotto and Nicolini (2007), Anderloni (1997), Johnson and Sullivan (1983), Johnson and Johnson (1998), Caskey (1994), Staten and Johnson (1995), DTI (2000), Villegas (1989), CGAP (2004), Fernando (2006), Davydoff and Naacke (2005).

[33] It was seen in Chap. 1 (Sect. 1.4) how financial education initiatives aimed at helping individuals make correct borrowing decisions only marginally affect behaviour patterns. In fact, due to the presence of psychological factors such as the availability heuristic and hyperbolic discounting factor, deviant behaviour patterns persist even when individuals are aware of the financial risks they run as a result of the consumption choices made. Indeed, increased awareness of the sanctions applied in cases of insolvency appears to act as a more effective deterrent (Kilborn 200; Watson 2003; Lea et al. 1995).

4.3 Policy Measures for the Prevention and Management of Over-Indebtedness

These measures currently exist only in those EU countries where consumer insolvency regulation is in place (Table 4.3[34]).

Debt settlement procedures offer debtors protection from the claims of single unsecured creditors and generally seek solutions that benefit both debtors and creditors.

These procedures generally include restructure plans and, in some cases, the cancellation of parts of a loan judged irrecoverable.

These ex post measures seek, on one hand, to provide help to individuals who find themselves in situations they can no longer sustain, also by cancelling part of the amounts owed (debt write-off) and, on the other, to prevent individuals' making their situation worse by resorting to illegal credit suppliers as a way of repaying debts contracted on formal credit markets. In this way, an individual has the chance to make a fresh start that otherwise would not be possible if future earnings were destined to extinguishing past debts.

Debt settlement procedures generally consist in two stages: out-of-court proceedings and court hearings.[35] Application to start procedures is usually made by the insolvent party and is generally accepted if the applicant can demonstrate his or her good faith or has not in the meantime worsened the situation by contracting further credit agreements.[36]

These procedures lead to a debt repayment plan agreed on by creditors. If no agreement can be found, the parties will go to court where it will be the judge who decides on a repayment plan that takes into account the insolvent party's living costs and those, where applicable, of his or her household along with a maximum time period in which the sums owed have to be repaid, normally 5 years.

When individuals' resources cannot cover basic living expenses and repayment instalments, the debt can, in certain cases, be frozen in order to enable insolvent parties to improve their economic and financial position before restarting payments.

---

[34]For detailed information on EU countries consumer insolvency regulation see the Appendix (Table 4.4).

[35]The connection between these two stages varies from country to country. For example, in France, Belgium, the Netherlands and Luxembourg the two procedures are identical and the only difference is that in the second case any decision has to be made by a judge. Vice-versa, in the United Kingdom out-of-court proceedings are completely separate from those held in court and are administered by private enterprises that receive a commission fee and whose responsibilities and operating standards are regulated by a specific Code of Practice. In Italy, at present, no individual debt settlement procedures exist, although two legislative proposals have been made in the last 2 years (no. 412 of 3rd May 2006 and no. 1811 of 25th September 2007). The Law accompanying the 2008 Budget (*Legge Finanziaria*) no. 244/2007 establishes a solidarity and support fund for those in difficulty paying mortgage instalments. This measure is, however, a one-off solution in response to the rising cost of floating-rate mortgages that has significantly increased the debt exposure of many Italian households.

[36]Access conditions applied to these procedures vary from country to country: in Finland, Sweden and Norway, for instance, courts can refuse debt settlement applications from individuals judged to have behaved irresponsibly, whilst in Germany and Austria applications are examined exclusively on economic grounds, such as the existence of sufficient resources to guarantee repayment as set down in repayment schedules, and not on the basis of individuals' behaviour (OEE, CESP, CRPF 2007; Niemi-Kiesilainen, Henrikson 2005).

Table 4.3 Consumer insolvency regulation in EU countries

Country	Law	Year
Austria	*Konkursordnung*	1995
Belgium	*Code Judiciaire/Gerechtelijk Wetboek/Judicial Code*	1998
Finland	Act on the Adjustment of the Debts of a Private Individual	1993
France	Consumer credit (L.333–1 to L.333–8)	1995
Germany	*Insolvenzordnung*	1994[a]
Greece	No	
Ireland	Bankruptcy Act	1988
Italy	No	
Latvia	No	
Lithuania	No	
Luxembourg	Law on overindebtedness	2000
Netherlands	Bankruptcy Act	1998
Portugal	No	
Slovenia	No	
Spain	No	
Sweden	Swedish Bankruptcy Act	1987
UK	Insolvency Act	1986

[a]adopted in 1999

Individuals or households without real or financial assets can in some cases benefit from the write-off of part of the debt according to terms already inserted in the procedure or added subsequently.[37]

The writing off of debt is nonetheless controversial because of the clear moral hazard implications.[38] It is important, however, to stress that such concessions can only be granted to individuals acting in good faith and can only be effective when inserted into a unitary set of measures aimed at preventing and managing over-indebtedness.

---

[37]In France, for example, cancellation of part of the total amount owed is foreseen by Law no. 701 of 11th August 2003 (*Loi Borloo*), which introduced reforms to previous legislation on the subject – Law no.1010 of 31st December 1989 (*Loi Neiertz*).

[38]The need to reduce total debt cancellations and related opportunistic behaviour by borrowers is currently the subject of debate in the United States. Debt cancellation is commonly used as part of bankruptcy proceedings: the writing off of the insolvent party's total liabilities is regarded as an important way of enabling a person in difficulty to make a fresh start. In the light, also, of the expansion in the use of consumer credit and related over-indebtedness, in some cases due to opportunistic behaviour by borrowers (Fay et al. 2002), the Bankruptcy Abuse Prevention and Consumer Protection Act of 2005 limits debt cancellation exclusively to individuals and households with no real or financial assets and no realistic prospects of future income.

Appendix

Table 4.4 Consumer insolvency regulation in EU countries: main contents

Country	Law	Main contents
Austria	*Konkursordnung* (Bankruptcy Code), section 25 "*Schuldenregulierungsverfahren*" (Debt settlement proceedings) Year: 1995	*Insolvency definition and proceedings admission*: A debtor may apply for composition proceedings to be opened if he is unable to pay or is over-indebted. Requirements: debtor's honesty, proposal for payment of the statutory minimum quota (40% of the creditors' claims) within 2 years following acceptance of the composition *Proceedings*: Amicable settlement. Extra-judicial attempt to set up consensual payment plan with creditors Judicial settlement. The proceeding can end up with cancellation without debtor supervision; cancellation with supervision by an administrator; continuation with supervision by the composition trustee. The option of exemption from residual debt is available if debtor pays at least 40% of the claims within 2 years. Maximum admissible payment term: 7 years
Belgium	*Code Judiciaire/Gerechtelijk Wetboek Judicial Code* (Judicial code), section "Collective Debt Arrangement" (1675/2–1675/19) Year: 1998	*Insolvency definition and proceedings admission*: For natural person the composition procedure is governed by the Judicial Code. Conditions for debtors to apply for composition are to be resident in Belgium and to be durably unable to pay debts *Proceedings:* Amicable settlement. Extra-judicial attempt to set up consensual payment plan with creditors Judicial settlement. The court can impose two plans: 1. The court defers or delay payments and reduces interest rates for up to 5 years; 2. The court discharges even the principal claims against the debtor Conditions for the discharge of the principal:

(*continued*)

Table 4.4 (continued)

Country	Law	Main contents
		– After the debtor has completed a three-to-five-year payment plan; – If some kind of five-year plan without a capital discharge would not allow the debtor to pay off his debts in full.
Finland	Act on the Adjustment of the Debts of a Private Individual, n.57 Year: 1993	*Insolvency definition and proceedings admission*: The procedure is open only to debtors who are insolvent and reasonably unable to improve his insolvency in order to discharge his debts. For the opening of the proceedings are also relevant: – The reasons for insolvency (i.e. unemployment, illness) – The absence of impediment in law to the debt adjustment proceedings (i.e. debt incurred through criminal activity or clearly negligent running up of debts) *Proceedings:* The debtor or liquidator draws up a proposed payment programme and creditors are offered the opportunity to comment on the proposed payment programme; a payment programme tailored to the debtor's genuine ability to pay is confirmed to the debtor as part of the adjustment proceedings. The payment programme is of a specified duration, generally 5 years. The payment programme covers all debts incurred prior to the opening of the proceeding, including secured debts Where a debtor fulfils the payment obligations confirmed in the payment programme, he is discharged from the rest of his debts A debtor in respect of whom an application for debt adjustment proceedings is pending cannot be declared bankrupt
France	Consumer credit (L.333–1 to L.333–8) Year: 1995	*Insolvency definition and proceedings admission*: A debtor is insolvent when it is impossible for him to meet current liabilities with the available assets. The conditions for natural persons opening the proceedings are good faith and the

(*continued*)

Appendix 93

Table 4.4 (continued)

Country	Law	Main contents
		manifest impossibility of paying all the debts
		Proceedings:
		Amicable settlement. When a debtor needs cannot be covered but has not yet reached a stage of cessation of payments, he may ask for an amicable settlement procedure. The president of the court then appoints a conciliator whose mission, which may not exceed 3 months, is to seek an agreement with the creditors. If the president approves the agreement, individual proceedings are suspended during the enforcement of the agreement
		Personal recovery proceedings. If the person can prove that his situation is irremediably compromised, he may apply to the court for the opening of personal recovery proceedings. The creditors are listed, the assets are evaluated and the judge orders the winding-up of the debtor's personal wealth. He appoints a liquidator to distribute the income from the assets among the creditors according to ranking
		If it is not possible to meet the debts of all the creditors, he declares the proceedings closed due to insufficient assets, which results in the erasing of the debtor's non-professional debts, with the exception of those paid by means of a guarantee
Germany	*Insolvenzordnung* (German Insolvency Regulation) Year: 1994	*Insolvency definition and proceedings admission*:
		In order to open insolvency proceedings the debtor has to be unable to make payment and/or be over-indebted. Inability to make payment exists if a debtor is not in a position to meet the payment obligations which are due; over-indebtedness exists if the debtor's assets no longer cover the existing obligations
		Proceedings:
		Amicable settlement. The debtor's primary obligation is to negotiate with creditors before and during the proceedings; he has to attach a complete payment proposal to the application. The court confirms the plan if it is accepted by

(*continued*)

Table 4.4 (continued)

Country	Law	Main contents
		a majority of the creditors or if there is no creditor opposition Insolvency proceedings. With the opening of the insolvency proceedings, the debtor's right to administer and dispose of the assets constituting the insolvency assets passes to the insolvency administrator. Moveable items required by the debtor for his livelihood are not covered by this "seizure"; employment income only forms part of the insolvency assets in as much as it exceeds the debtor's minimum subsistence level Insolvency proceedings allow natural persons a financial fresh start which is achieved by discharge of remaining debts, that is any debts which have not yet been paid off after the conclusion of the insolvency proceeding
Ireland	Bankruptcy Act Year: 1988	*Insolvency definition and proceedings admission*: Condition for opening insolvency proceedings are the commission of an Act of Bankruptcy and an amount of debt to be liquidated not less than 2,000 euros *Proceedings:* Pre-insolvency proceedings: – Bankruptcy summons, which requires payment of the sum due within 14 days in default of which the debtor will have committed an act of Bankruptcy – Petition for arrangement. The debtor can petition the court for protection from bankruptcy proceeding so that he can put an offer of composition to his creditors. If the offer is accepted by three-fifths in number and value of his creditors and approved by the Court then it is binding on all his creditors Insolvency proceedings: if the offer is not accepted or not approved by the Court then the Court itself may adjudicate the debtor Bankrupt
Luxemburg	Law on over-indebtedness, section "Collective debt settlement procedure Year: 2000	*Insolvency definition and proceedings admission*: The procedure is open only to insolvent natural persons who are not traders, who have not become insolvent deliberately

(*continued*)

Table 4.4 (continued)

Country	Law	Main contents
		and who are legally resident in Luxembourg
		Proceedings:
		Amicable settlement. The *Service d'information et de Conseil en surendettement* (Over- indebtedness Information and Advice Service) will examine the file and draw up a draft recovery plan in agreement with the debtor and his creditors
		This draft will be submitted to the Mediation Commission, which will in turn propose a recovery plan to the debtor and the creditors, containing measures ranging from merely postponing or rescheduling debt payments to cancelling all or part of the debt
		Judicial settlement. The parties will be summoned before the magistrate's court, which may require them to submit all the documents and information enabling the court to establish the debtor's assets and liabilities
		On the basis of this information, the court will decide on a recovery plan containing measures which will enable the debtor to meet his commitments
		The recovery plan adopted by the court will be valid for a maximum of 7 years and may be rendered null and void in a limited number of cases (i.e. where the debtor does not meet the obligations imposed on him by the recovery plan)
Netherlands	Bankruptcy Act, section 284 "Debt Restructuring for Natural person act" Year: 1998	*Insolvency definition and proceedings admission*:
		A debtor is insolvent when he has ceased to make payments. An insolvent debtor who is a natural person can apply for a debt restructuring procedure
		Proceedings:
		Amicable settlement. Prior to application of the legal debt restructuring arrangement, the law imposes mandatory pursuit of an extrajudicial phase: it must be evident that there have been attempts to reach an amicable settlement and why these attempts have been in vain. The debt assistance provision at a local level supports this amicable phase

(*continued*)

Table 4.4 (continued)

Country	Law	Main contents
		Debt restructuring arrangement. When a debtor applies for a debt restructuring the following has to occur: – An incurable debt burden must be involved – He must enclose a model statement with the restructuring application – The debts must have arisen or remained unpaid in good faith (i.e. no debt from criminal acts) The debtor who is admitted to debt restructuring should exert maximum effort for his creditors for a period of 3 years, during which he will have to make his capacity to repay available to his creditors up to 95% of the applicable support level If a remission of debts is provided to the debtor on completion of debt restructuring, it applies to all creditors, even to individuals who have not submitted their claim to the receiver. If the debtor does not adhere to his debt restructuring obligations, he will be lawfully in a state of bankruptcy
Sweden	Swedish Bankruptcy Act Year: 1987	*Insolvency definition and proceedings admission*: A debtor is insolvent when he is unable to pay his debts in a proper manner where such inability is not temporary. The person must be resident in Sweden, he must be so deeply in debt that he cannot be expected to be able to pay his debts in the foreseeable future *Proceedings:* Amicable settlement. They are arrangements that are not specifically regulated by law but are treated in the same way as other forms of agreement Debt restructuring (*skuldsanering*). All debts covered by the procedure are reduced or eliminated since a debt restructuring decision will include the proportion of the debt the debtor must pay. It will also include a payment plan which normally runs for 5 years Under the payment plan the debtor whose debts have been restructured must live on the minimum subsistence amount. If the

(*continued*)

Appendix   97

Table 4.4 (continued)

Country	Law	Main contents
		debtor has no income over and above the minimum subsistence amount he or she does not have to pay anything
United Kindgom	Insolvency Act Year: 1986	*Insolvency definition and proceedings admission*: A debtor is insolvent if he has insufficient assets to meet all debts, or he is unable to pay debts when they are due *Proceedings:* Amicable settlement. Individuals can enter into informal arrangements with their creditors to accept less than the full amount they are owed; such arrangements are not binding Individual voluntary agreements (IVA) Any debtor owing more than £15,000 in unsecured debts has the opportunity to apply for an IVA. An IVA is a new agreement between the debtor and all unsecured creditors to make a revised monthly payment in satisfaction of all previous debt obligations for a period of 60 months In order to obtain an IVA at least 75% of the creditors have to approve the proposals put forward by the debtor. Once approved the arrangement is binding on all creditors who received notice of the proposals The agreement will stop further interest and charges. Moreover, an amount of debt will usually be written off at the end of the IVA and bankruptcy is avoided

Chapter 5
Regulatory Framework

5.1 Introduction

The regulation of consumer credit in Europe derives from a variety of sources both at EU and national levels (laws, regulations and administrative provisions), many of which are responses in the course of time to emerging regulatory needs.[1]

The adoption of the first Consumer Credit Directive[2] certainly acted as a significant driver at national level for legislative intervention in those countries without specific consumer credit laws as well as for rationalisation and reform in countries with existing and differing frameworks.

In the years that followed, expansion in the supply and variety of credit forms allied to strong demand from consumers meant a series of legislative updates and amendments until the radical, wide-ranging reforms contained in the new Consumer Credit Directive.[3]

In this chapter we will examine the principal changes contained in the new Directive and how these will affect lenders' activities and their relations with customers.

---

[1] Examples include provisions adopted to prevent money laundering and terrorist funding as well as measures aimed at regulating the use of personal data.

[2] See Directive 87/102/EEC of December 1986 for the approximation of the laws, regulations and administrative provisions of the Member States concerning consumer credit, in Official Journal L 042, 12th February 1987.

[3] See Directive 2008/48/EC of the European Parliament and of the Council of 23rd April 2008 on credit agreements for consumers and repealing Council Directive 87/102/EEC in Official Journal of the European Union, 22nd May 2008. Member States should adopt and apply the provisions necessary to comply with the new Directive at least before 12th May 2010. The need for regulatory overhaul is pointed out at the "whereas (5)": "In recent years the types of credit offered to and used by consumers have evolved considerably. New credit instruments have appeared, and their use continues to develop. It is therefore necessary to amend existing provisions and to extend their scope, where appropriate".

5.2 The New Consumer Credit Directive

Work on revising the first Consumer Credit Directive of 1986 began in 2002 on the back of changes to national consumer credit markets that had made the first Directive,[4] already amended in 1990[5] and 1998,[6] no longer equipped to handle a changed market environment.

The review process leading to the new Directive was long and complex and consisted of a series of stop and go consultations before the final approval. The new Directive reflects the need to reconcile not only differing national positions – which represented competitive distortions within the single market and produced barriers to its proper working which effectively limited the possibility for consumers to make cross-border choices[7] – but also at times conflicting interests of major stakeholders (banks, non banking financial intermediaries, consumers and consumer associations, a plethora of regulatory and oversight bodies in the areas of financial services, monetary policy, competition and personal data, etc.).[8]

Despite some inevitable weaknesses, the new Directive is an important step towards the creation of a more efficient and transparent single European consumer credit market characterised also by cross-border activities.[9]

The Directive seeks to both strengthen and broaden the harmonisation process started in 1986. In fact, while the first Directive sought about a certain degree of approximation of consumer credit law as well as providing measures to protect consumers, the new Directive seeks to push towards full harmonisation, at least in

---

[4]The first Directive (87/102/EEC) was passed at a time when, especially in some countries, the use of consumer credit was still limited and the forms in which it was granted were comparatively simple. With the aim of creating a single consumer credit market and establishing a minimum shared framework of consumer protection, the 1986 Directive established only certain basic principles to be respected and left individual Member States the opportunity to introduce more restrictive legislation where necessary. Such an approach over time generated marked cross-country differences, above all in the area of consumer protection, which in turn led to distortions both in terms of competition amongst EU lenders and consumers' access to cross-border credit.

[5]See Council Directive 90/88/EEC of 22nd February 1990 amending Directive 87/102/EEC for the approximation of the laws, regulations and administrative provisions of the Member States concerning consumer credit, Official Journal L 61 14 10.3.1990.

[6]See Directive 98/7/EC of the European Parliament and of the Council of 16th February 1998 amending Directive 87/102/EEC for the approximation of the laws, regulations and administrative provisions of the Member States concerning consumer credit, Official Journal L 101, 01/04/1998.

[7]See Whereas (4), Directive 2008/48/EC, which draws attention also to the fact that "Those distortions and restrictions may in turn have consequences in terms of the demand for goods and services".

[8]An analysis of the problem areas and weak points connected to the new Directive, which entails a detailed assessment of current legislation in force across the EU, is outside the scope of this chapter. For an analysis of the difficulties faced in carrying out such an assessment, see Oxera (2007), whilst for criticisms of the Directive see the position papers of the House of Lords (2006), Sveriges Konsumentrad (2006), European Commission (2005), European Financial Services round table (2006).

[9]Directive 2008/48/EC, at Whereas (6) and (7).

5.2 The New Consumer Credit Directive

a number of core areas, that guarantees all EU consumers the possibility to enjoy uniform and high levels of protection within a single consumer credit market.[10]

So-called "full" harmonisation refers exclusively to certain aspects of the laws, regulations and administrative provisions of the Member States concerning agreements covering credit for consumers. Consequently, as regards areas harmonised, Member States should not be allowed to maintain or introduce national provisions. Viceversa, where no such harmonised provisions exist, Member States should remain free to maintain or introduce national legislation.[11]

In fact, in reviewing existing Community legislation, the Commission identified key priority areas that required intervention, whilst leaving other matters to be handled by national legislation, if already in place. As a result of this review, the main objective was, therefore, to raise the transparency and efficiency of the consumer credit market so that consumers are in a position to assess differing credit products, also from other Member States, on the basis of a uniform set of features. Such an approach places consumer protection in the forefront by providing for the full disclosure of the rights a consumer is entitled to enjoy throughout the life of the credit agreement. Compliance with these provisions is also foreseen by providing that implementation of the Directive "cannot be circumvented as a result of the way in which agreements are formulated".[12]

Moreover, whilst the focus of the first Directive was mainly on the needs of the demand side, i.e. consumer protection, the new Directive marks a decisive attempt to address the needs also of the supply side.[13] In fact, considerable importance is given to the need for a regulatory environment that does not generate competitive distortions amongst consumer credit lenders and which acts as an incentive to cross-border lending.

The Directive's objective is therefore to harmonise fully core areas relating to consumer credit contracts so as to, on one hand, promote the development of cross-border consumer credit through the conduit of an internal market without internal frontiers and, on the other, ensure that EU consumers are able to benefit from a high and equivalent level of protection of their interests.[14]

---

[10] Directive 2008/48/EC at Whereas (9).

[11] Consequently, Member States may, for example, maintain or introduce national provisions regarding joint and several liability of the seller or the service provider and the creditor. A further example of this possibility for Member States could be the maintenance or introduction of national provisions regarding the cancellation of a contract for the sale of goods or supply of services if the consumer exercises his right of withdrawal from the credit agreement. On this question, Member States, in the case of open-end credit agreements, should be allowed to fix a minimum period from the time when the creditor asks for reimbursement and the day on which the credit has to be reimbursed.

[12] Article 22 (3) and (4).

[13] Whereas (4)–(9).

[14] Whereas (4)–(9).

These objectives will be reached via regulation of the following areas:

- Information[15]
- Assessment of households' creditworthiness[16]
- Rights concerning credit agreements[17]
- Creditors and credit intermediaries[18]

5.3 Information Requirements for Consumer Credit Agreements

Information requirements undoubtedly represent the foundation for regulation as they were in the first Directive's attempts to improve levels of disclosure regarding credit products and thereby help consumers make informed decisions.[19]

The new Consumer Credit Directive sets out informational requirements across four distinct stages: information to be included in advertising;[20] pre-contractual information;[21] information to be included in credit agreements;[22] information to be provided after the signing of the credit agreement.[23]

Irrespective of any particular stage, information is characterised by two particular features: it has to be, firstly, clear and concise and, secondly, useable over time.

As regards the first requirement, the Directive states at article 4 that standard information shall specify a variety of elements "in a clear, concise and prominent way", whilst article 10 prescribes that the information to be included in credit agreements be specified "in a clear and concise manner". Along with a breakdown of the specific elements to be included in the agreement, it covers other content features such as a Standard European Consumer Credit Information format and the equation establishing the annual percentage rate of charge (APR).

The feature of information durability is guaranteed by the fact that credit agreements shall be drawn up on paper or "another durable medium".[24]

---

[15] See articles 4–7,10–12,18–19.

[16] See articles 8–9.

[17] See articles 13–17.

[18] See articles 20–21.

[19] The role information plays in decisions regarding indebtedness were discussed in Chap. 4. There is little doubt that transparent, correct and comprehensive information is fundamental in enabling the consumer to make an informed decision. It must be pointed out, however, that the emphasis should be on quality rather than quantity. Indeed, a disclosure overload may prove to be a hindrance rather than a help.

[20] See article 4.

[21] See articles 5–6–7–8–9.

[22] See article 10.

[23] See articles 11–12–13–14–15–16–17–18.

[24] This means "any instrument which enables the consumer to store information addressed personally to him in a way accessible for future reference for a period of time adequate for the purposes of information and which allows the unchanged reproduction of the information stored".

Having identified the informational requirements to be met, we are now in a better position to see how the contents of the credit agreements are to be regulated.

5.3.1 Advertising

The Directive establishes the minimum informational elements to be included in advertising concerning credit agreements. This "standard information", summarised in Table 5.1, is intended as a set of defined elements (article 3 provides a list of definitions of the various elements making up the credit agreement) necessary for the consumer to compare different offers and reach an informed decision.[25] Understanding and comparing information is helped by the supply of "representative examples".

Turning to the supply side, the standardisation of information to be provided during the advertising stage should raise lenders' competitiveness also in a cross-border context by enabling them to operate from a homogeneous product content platform.

Standard information and mandatory disclosure requirements are not, however, intended to create excessively mechanical or bureaucratic relations between lenders and their customers. In fact, the Directive invites EU Member States to legislate to ensure that creditors and their credit intermediaries provide adequate explanations in order to place the consumer in a position in which he/she can assess whether the product on offer is appropriate to individual needs and financial situation. With this in mind, standard information should provide details of the "essential characteristics of the products proposed and the special effects they may have, including the consequences of default in payment by the consumer".[26] In line with the spirit of subsidiarity, the procedures chosen to implement the Directive's provisions should be flexible enough to capture needs and problem areas without creating excessive bureaucracy.

5.3.2 Pre-Contractual Information

In the pre-contractual stage, the new Directive establishes even more rigid qualitative levels with standard information being provided by means of the "Standard

---

[25]More specifically, the borrowing rate, the total amount of credit, the annual percentage rate of charge and, if applicable, the duration of the credit agreement, the cash price and amount of advance payment in the case of credit for deferred payment on goods or services and the total amount payable by the consumer and the amount of instalments.

[26]See article 5, subparagraph 6.

European Consumer Credit Information form",[27] with other specific forms foreseen for overdraft facilities, and for certain specific credit agreements.[28]

As part of its regulation of standard consumer credit agreements, pre-contractual information is broken down into five sections: (1) identity and contact details of the credit providers or credit intermediaries,[29] (2) description of the main features of the credit product, (3) costs of the credit, (4) other important legal aspects, and (5) additional information in the case of distance marketing of financial services.

Certain items in each section in italics explain either the meaning of an item ("This means..."), draw attention to consumer rights (i.e. "You have the right to withdraw from the credit agreement within a period of 14 calendar days" and "You have the right to repay the credit early at any time in full or partially") or raise awareness of consumer risks (i.e. "Missing payment could have severe consequences for you (i.e. forced sale) and make obtaining credit more difficult"). Square brackets are used to indicate explanations the creditor requires and which must be provided (i.e. "You will have to pay the following: [The amount, number and frequency of payments to be made by the customer]").

The Standard European Consumer Credit Information form shall be on paper or another durable medium so as to enable the consumer to access it for future reference.[30]

The disclosure requirements regarding the rights and duties of both parties to the credit agreement are, as indicated above, flanked by explanations and warnings regarding certain conditions contained in the contract. The aim here is clearly to promote responsible borrowing behaviour on the part of consumers. The mandatory disclosure of pre-contractual information in the form and medium described above

---

[27] The form is reproduced in the Appendix at Table 5.5.

[28] See article 7. There are other, albeit minor, cases which pursuant to the Directive are to be considered as specific: one is the case of credit agreements under which payments made by the consumer "do not give rise to an immediate corresponding amortisation of the total amount of credit, but are used to constitute capital during periods and under conditions laid down in the credit agreement or in an ancillary agreement" (article 10, subparagraph 4).

[29] For a description of the various credit supply-side players, see Sect. 5.6.

[30] In the case of voice telephony communications, the Directive states pre-contractual requirements shall be regulated by the provisions of Directive 2002/65/EC concerning the distance marketing of consumer financial services and amending Council Directive 90/619/EEC and Directives 97/7/EC and 98/27/EC. Information to be provided concerns the main characteristics of the financial service "together with the annual percentage rate illustrated by means of a representative example and the total amount payable by the consumer" (article 5, subparagraph 2). Furthermore, if the agreement has been concluded at the consumer's request using a means of distance communication such as voice telephony, the creditor "shall provide the consumer with the full pre-contractual information using the Standard European Consumer Credit Information form immediately after the conclusion of the credit agreement" (article 5, subparagraph 3). The following paragraph provides for increased consumer protection, providing that the consumer shall on request, receive together with the Standard European Credit Information, a copy of the draft credit agreement free of charge. This provision shall not apply "if the creditor is at the time of the request unwilling to proceed to the conclusion of the agreement with the consumer" (article 5, subparagraph 4).

5.3 Information Requirements for Consumer Credit Agreements

can be clearly inferred from article 5, which states that the Standard European Consumer Credit Information form shall be provided to the consumer "in good time before the consumer is bound by any credit agreement or offer" in order that the consumer is provided with "the information needed to compare different offers in order to take an informed decision on whether to conclude a credit agreement". Any additional information the creditor wishes to provide the consumer shall be given in a separate document that may be annexed to the Standard European Consumer Credit Information form.

5.3.2.1 The Annual Percentage Rate

With the aim of helping customers to compare different offers, in the pre-contractual stage and more in general in the new Directive considerable attention is placed on information related to the costs of credit and, in particular, APR.

The APR, along with the requirement that the agreement shall be drawn up on paper, was introduced by the first Consumer Credit Directive. Both features represented a landmark in the regulation of consumer credit, which for the first time identified consumer protection and a harmonised European consumer credit market as its objectives. To achieve these goals, homogeneous comparatives were needed to evaluate different products offered in different countries often priced on the basis of different methods. Having established the usefulness of reference points such as the "total cost of credit to the consumer"[31] and the "annual percentage rate of charge",[32] specific methods adopted to calculate both were to be fixed initially in accordance with the provisions or practices existing in the Member States or, eventually, to be established freely by each of them. In other words, countries were given freedom to regulate the question on the basis of existing approaches and legislation. Efforts to harmonise instruments that were at that time not in widespread use among the majority of EU Member States would not have been justified.

At the beginning of the 1990s, the decision to adopt one method in calculating APR represented another step towards harmonisation and the creation of an internal market in which consumers may benefit from high levels of protection. As a result, a single mathematical formula was introduced for calculating the APR and for determining credit cost items to be used in the calculation by indicating those costs which must not be taken into account[33]. Later, in 1998, Directive 98/7/EC reformulated APR as such: "The annual percentage rate of charge which shall be that rate, on an annual basis which equalizes the present value of all commitments

---

[31]Defined as "All the costs of the credit, including interest and other charges directly connected with the credit agreement", see article 1 (d), Directive 87/102/EC.

[32]Defined as "The total cost of the credit to the consumer expressed as an annual percentage of the amount of the credit granted", see article 1(e), Directive 87/102/EC.

[33]See Council Directive 90/88/EEC of 22nd February 1990 amending Directive 87/102/EEC for the approximation of the laws, regulations and administrative provisions of the Member States concerning consumer credit, article 1 and annexes.

(loans, repayments and charges), future or existing, agreed by the creditor and the borrower, shall be calculated in accordance with the mathematical formula set out in Annex II"; the same Directive also made provisions that raised the level of information to be included in the advertising and offer of credit agreements.[34]

After a lengthy review process and the partial acceptance of demands from the credit supply side and the wider acceptance of requests from policy makers and consumer organisations, the terms and mathematical formula were revised. The aim of this revision was to enable the consumer to compare different credit proposals and decide in full knowledge of the facts relating to the costs of the loan.[35]

Although the definition of APR remains unchanged as "the total cost of the credit to the consumer, expressed as an annual percentage of the total amount of credit", the notion of "total cost of the credit to the consumer" is defined, in more detail than in the past, as: "All the costs, including interest, commissions, taxes and any other kind of fees which the consumer is required to pay in connection with the credit agreement and which are known to the creditor, except for notarial costs; costs in respect of ancillary services relating to the credit agreement, in particular insurance premiums, are also included if, in addition, the conclusion of a service contract is compulsory in order to obtain the credit or to obtain it on the terms and conditions marketed". Consequently, the calculation of the total cost must include the costs of maintaining an account recording both payment transactions and drawdowns and the costs of using a means of payment for both payment transactions and drawdowns; other costs relating to payment transactions shall be included in the total cost of credit to the consumer unless the opening of the account is optional and the costs of the account have been clearly and separately shown in the credit agreement or in any other agreement concluded with the consumer.[36]

The basic equation, which establishes APR, equates on an annual basis the present value of all commitments (drawdowns, repayments and charges), future or existing, agreed by the creditor and the consumer:

$$\sum_{k=1}^{m} C_k (1+X)^{-t_k} = \sum_{l=1}^{m'} D_l (1+X)^{-t_l}$$

where:

–   X is the APR
–   m is the number of the last drawdown

---

[34]See Directive 98/7/EC of the European Parliament and of the council of 16th February 1998, article 1 and annexes.

[35]Whereas (43) states that "Despite the uniform mathematical formula for its calculation, the annual percentage rate of charge provided for in Directive 87/102/EEC is not yet fully comparable throughout the Community. In individual Member States different cost factors are taken into account in the calculation thereof. This Directive should therefore clearly and comprehensively define the total cost of a credit to the consumer".

[36]See article 19(2).

5.3 Information Requirements for Consumer Credit Agreements

- k is the number of a drawdown, thus $1 \leq k \leq m$
- C_k is the amount of drawdown k
- t_k is the interval, expressed in years and fractions of a year, between the date of the first drawdown and the date of each subsequent drawdown, thus $t_1 = 0$
- m' is the number of the last repayment or payment of charges
- l is the number of a repayment or payment of charges
- D_l is the amount of a repayment or payment of charges
- s_l is the interval, expressed in years and fractions of a year, between the date of the first drawdown and the date of each repayment or payment of charges

The formula is followed by a series of remarks that provide further details as to starting rate, the form in which intervals between dates used in the calculation are to be expressed, along with additional assumptions for the calculation of the APR covering a wide area of cases and uses.[37]

Unlike in the past, the illustrative examples for calculation of the APR as foreseen in former Annex III have been omitted in view of the Commission's overall target of better regulation and in order not to over-burden the legislative procedure.

Significantly, the Directive addresses the risk that the assumptions outlined in Annex I for calculating APR are no longer suitable due to changes in the market scenario. In fact, the Commission, assisted by a Committee (an example of the so-called comitology approach), may make any additions or changes necessary.[38]

The legislative review procedure inevitably consists of an extensive and time-consuming consultation process with the multiple stakeholders involved, in addition to an evaluation of the impact changes in the law will have on the sector and its players. The approach adopted in the case of APR is a welcome attempt by the Commission to heighten the market effectiveness of the legislation and to ensure that it does not represent an obstacle to product and operating innovation in the consumer credit sector.

---

[37] (1) The amounts paid by both parties at different times shall not necessarily be equal and shall not necessarily be paid at equal intervals; (2) The starting date shall be that of the first drawdown; (3) Intervals between dates used in the calculations shall be expressed in years or in fractions of a year. A year is presumed to have 365 days (or 366 days for leap years), 52 weeks or 12 equal months. An equal month is presumed to have 30.4 days (i.e. 365/12) regardless of whether or not it is a leap year; (4) The result of the calculation shall be expressed with an accuracy of at least one decimal place. If the figure at the following decimal place is greater than or equal to 5, the figure at that particular decimal place shall be increased by one. (5) The equation can be rewritten using a single sum and the concept of flows (Ak), which will be positive or negative, in other words either paid or received during periods 1-k, expressed in years, i.e.

$$S = \sum_{k=1}^{n} A_k (1+X)^{-t_k}$$

S being the present balance of flows. If the aim is to maintain the equivalence of flows, the value will be zero.

[38] Article 19(5).

5.3.3 Information to be Included in the Credit Agreement

Information to be included in the credit agreement aims to provide the consumer with clear details of the credit terms and conditions as well as the existence or absence of certain rights. The contents of the pre-contractual phase as specified in the Standard European Consumer Credit form are carried over into the agreement itself. Article 10 reiterates these in addition to stating additional information requirements such as a statement of account in the form of an amortisation table to be made available to the consumer on request for fixed duration loans. In this way the consumer can monitor capital amortisation, the interest calculated on the basis of the borrowing rate applied and any additional costs.[39] In the case of charges and interest payable without capital amortisation, the statement of account shall show the periods and conditions for the payment of interest and charges.

Considerable attention is also placed on the consumer's rights relating to withdrawal, early repayment, and the existence of out-of-court complaint and redress mechanisms. These rights will be discussed in paragraph 5.5 below.

As appears clear from Table 5.1, the new Directive has raised significantly the quantitative and qualitative levels of information to be included in credit agreements. The first Directive, in fact, stated only that "the written agreement shall further include other essential terms of the contract"[40] and provided examples of these minimal requirements in a specific annex. Nevertheless, the first Directive represented an important step in leading off the improvement of consumer protection levels via more complete and transparent information throughout every stage of the consumer credit agreement.

5.3.4 Information to be Provided Throughout the Duration of the Contract

As regards the information requirements to be met throughout the duration of the contract, in addition to the consumer's right to demand an amortisation table, the creditor is also obliged to inform the consumer of changes in interest rates applied to variable-rate loans along with any resulting changes in the total amount of the credit, the number and frequency of payments, again on paper or another durable medium.[41] Where a credit agreement covers credit in the form of an overdraft

---

[39] See article 10, subparagraph 2, points (a)-(v).

[40] Directive 87/102/EEC, artiche 4, subparagraph 3.

[41] In the case of index-linked agreements, article 11, paragraph 2 states that the parties may agree that information relating to changes in the borrowing rate following a change in a reference rate is to be given to the consumer periodically and that "the new reference rate is to be made publicly available by appropriate means and the information concerning the new reference rate is also kept available in the premises of the creditor".

5.3 Information Requirements for Consumer Credit Agreements

Table 5.1 Differences between the first and the new Consumer Credit Directive: information requirements

	Directive 87/102/EEC as amended	Directive 2008/48/EC
Advertising	Any advertisement or any offer which is displayed at business premises, in which a person offers credit or offers to arrange a credit agreement and in which a rate of interest or any figures relating to the cost of the credit are indicated, shall also include a statement of APR, by means of a representative example if no other means is practicable (see article 3).	Any advertising concerning credit agreements which indicate an interest rate or any figures relating to the cost of the credit to the consumer shall include standard information that shall specify the borrowing rate, the total amount of credit, APR, the duration of the agreement (if applicable), the cash price and the amount of any advance payment (in the case of credit in the form of deferred payment for a specific good or service), the total amount payable by the consumer and the amount of the instalments (if applicable) If the conclusion of a contract regarding an ancillary service is compulsory (i.e. insurance) and the cost of that service cannot be determined in advance, the obligation to enter into the contract shall be stated in a clear, concise and prominent way, together with the annual percentage rate (see article 4)
Pre-contractual information	= = = = =	Article 5 states that information needed to compare different offers in order to take agreement shall be provided by means of the Standard European Consumer Credit Information and specifies the information contained in the Information form Article 6 states pre-contractual requirements for certain credit agreements (i.e. overdraft facilities)

(*continued*)

Table 5.1 (continued)

	Directive 87/102/EEC as amended	Directive 2008/48/EC
Information to be included in the credit agreement	Credit agreements shall be made in writing and shall include a statement of APR or of the condition under which APR may be amended and other essential terms (see article 4 and Appendix)	Article 10 states information to be included in credit agreements, among which amortisation table, interest rate in case of default, information concerning consumers' rights; article 11 states information concerning the borrowing rate and article 12 states information concerning overdraft facilities
Information to be provided throughout the duration of the contract	= = = = =	The creditor shall make available to the consumer, free of charge and at any time throughout the duration of the credit, a statement of account in the form of an amortisation table (see article 10). As regards borrowing rate, when the change in the borrowing rate is caused by a change in a reference rate, the new reference rate shall be made publicly available by appropriate means and the information concerning the new reference rate be also kept available in the premises of the creditor (see article 11) In the case of overdraft facilities, the creditor shall provide regular information by means of a statement account (see article 12)

5.3 Information Requirements for Consumer Credit Agreements

facility, the consumer shall be kept regularly informed by means of a statement of account, on paper or another durable medium, of any changes in the borrowing rate before the new rate comes into force.

Here, too, the new Directive seeks to provide consumers with the information necessary for them to monitor effectively their credit commitments and modify them if necessary.

The principal difference between the first and the new Directive lies not only in the increased quantity of information consumer credit lenders have to provide under the latter Directive, but also in the value this information has in helping households make responsible borrowing decisions.

The mandatory information that enables consumers to assess more easily and more effectively the impact debt will have on future financial flows has, however, already been anticipated in some European legislations.[42]

In France,[43] Belgium,[44] Germany[45] and the United Kingdom,[46] for instance, creditors are already obliged by law to send borrowers an amortisation table summarising the amounts (capital and interest) paid and those outstanding. In order to raise awareness of the financial risks arising from default, consumers in the same countries must also be informed at the pre-contractual and agreement stages of the costs incurred in case of insolvency.

Another feature of mature credit markets is the regulation of unfair and misleading advertising that may lead consumers to irresponsible borrowing decisions. In Belgium, for example, the advertising of interest-free credit is prohibited along with language that emphasises the speed and ease of access to credit (article 6, paragraphs 1 and 2). The same article also prohibits advertising that encourages consumers in financial difficulties to use further forms of credit to cover existing debt commitments.

The advertising of interest-free credit is also regulated in Ireland.[47] Article 25 of the Consumer Credit Act states that "an advertisement shall not describe credit as being without interest, or any other charge, if the availability of the credit is dependent on the consumer concluding with the creditor or any other person a maintenance contract or an insurance contract or on any other condition, compliance with which would, or would be likely in the future to, involve the consumer in any cost additional to that payable if the goods were bought for cash". Advertising aiming to compare the level of repayments or cost under one or more forms of financial accommodation is also regulated.

---

[42] The Second Directive introduces several new features in comparison to its predecessor. However, when comparing the new Directive with legislation passed at national level in certain EU Member States since 1986, one can see that certain provisions have already been anticipated.

[43] *Loi 78–22 sul crédit à la consommation* 10th January 1978.

[44] *Loi du 12th juin 1991 sur le crédit à la consummation.*

[45] *Verbraucherkreditgesetz* 17th December 1990.

[46] Consumer Credit Act 1974–2006.

[47] Consumer Credit Act 1995.

In France, the law prohibits advertising that suggests a loan can be obtained without providing information regarding the applicant's credit rating or which gives the impression that the liquidity provided comes without a financial commitment.

In the United Kingdom, consumer credit advertising is closely regulated by the Consumer Credit (Advertisements) Regulation 2004 as amended in 2007. As regards the expression "interest-free credit", article 4, paragraph 3 states that "an advertisement may not include the expression 'interest free' or any similar expression indicating that customers buying on credit may pay no more than they would as cash buyers, except where the total amount payable does not exceed the cash price". The same article provides that all costs shall appear on the same page or part of the page so that they are likely to be read as a whole.

5.4 Assessment of Creditworthiness

One area in which the new Directive differs significantly from its predecessor is in the mandatory assessment of the loan applicant's creditworthiness. This evaluation shall be based on information provided by the applicant or, if necessary, on the basis of consultation of specific databases.

The use of databases for the monitoring of credit quality is already established practice amongst banks and other mainstream credit providers subject to prudential regulation and oversight. However, in the case of lenders that target higher-risk customer segments attracted by the promise of quick, hassle-free loans, the Directive's provisions will represent for many a significant change.

The Directive in its preamble seeks to promote responsible practices during all phases of the credit relationship, starting with careful assessment of creditworthiness prior to the granting of the credit and awareness on the part of the borrower of the commitments involved in taking out the loan. In support of these objectives, information and education play an important role and include warnings about the risks attached to default and over-indebtedness. In fact, the Directive declares the following: "In the expanding credit market, in particular, it is important that creditors should not engage in irresponsible lending or give out credit without prior assessment of creditworthiness, and the Member States should carry out the necessary supervision to avoid such behaviour and should determine the necessary means to sanction creditors in the event of their doing so".[48]

Responsible lending here includes providing an unsuccessful applicant with the reasons why the request for a loan was turned down and by so doing help the prospective borrower understand his/her financial situation better. If the decision to reject an application is based on information provided by a database, the applicant should be informed of the fact and the reasons for rejections. Creditors are not obliged to provide such information when this is prohibited by Community or

---
[48]Whereas (26).

5.4 Assessment of Creditworthiness

Table 5.2 Differences between the first and the new Consumer Credit Directive: assessment of consumer creditworthiness

	Directive 87/102/EEC as amended	Directive 2008/48/EC
Creditworthiness of the consumer	= = = = = = =	Member States shall ensure that the creditor assesses the consumer's creditworthiness on the basis of sufficient information, both obtained from the consumer and, where necessary, on the basis of a consultation of the relevant database (see article 8)
Database access	= = = = =	Member States shall in the case of cross-border credit ensure access for creditors from other Member States to databases used in that Member State for assessing the creditworthiness of consumers at non-discriminatory conditions. If the credit application is rejected on the basis of consultation of a database, the creditor shall inform the consumer immediately and without charge of the result of such consultation and of the particulars of the database consulted (see article 9)

national legislation or when providing such information would be contrary to public security.[49]

The Directive in this area recognises the needs of the supply side by stating that, in order to avoid competitive distortions, access shall be ensured for "creditors from other Member States to databases used in that Member State for assessing the creditworthiness of consumers" and that "the conditions for access shall be non-discriminatory"[50] (Table 5.2).

Regulation already in place in some Member States specifically addresses the questions of responsible lending and the assessment of creditworthiness. In Belgium, for instance, article 10 of the *Loi sur le crédit à la consommation* requires lenders to ask applicants for details of other loan exposures they may have in addition to any details necessary for a correct assessment of creditworthiness. Article 12 also requires lenders to provide applicants with details of the credit bureau used in the case of an unsuccessful loan application. In the United Kingdom, provisions relating to credit assessment procedures, refusal of loan applications and the use of credit reference agencies are contained in specific self-regulation codes (Banking Code and Financial Leasing Association lending Code).[51]

---

[49] The use of databases for assessing consumer creditworthiness must be in accordance with the provisions relating to the protection and free movement of personal data processing contained in Directive 95/46/EC of the European Parliament and of the Council of 24th October 1995.

[50] See Chap. III, Article 9, "Database Access".

[51] Members subject to the provisions of the two Codes account for around 90% of unsecured lending in the UK. The remaining 10% is made up by lenders operating principally in the sub-prime market, a segment in which responsible lending is crucial in containing over-indebtedness. See Kempson (2008).

5.5 Protection of Other Consumer Rights

The objective of creating a level playing field for lenders and borrowers alike depends to a great extent on establishing consumer rights. The Directive makes detailed provisions regarding the rights the consumer should enjoy at all stages of the consumer agreement along with those foreseen in six situations. These are identified at Chap. 4 "Information and rights concerning credit agreements" as open-end credit agreements, right of withdrawal, linked credit agreements, early repayment, assignment of rights, and overrunning.

The existence of these rights and the manner in which they can be enforced are both strengthened by their inclusion in the Standard European Consumer Credit Information form, which, as we saw in Sect. 5.3.2, provides an explanation of the meaning of contract terms and specifies information to be supplied by the creditor.

Table 5.3 summarises differences between the first and the new Directive in this area. At this stage, we will examine briefly the areas stated in Chap. 4.

As regards the first, the consumer may effect standard termination of an open-end agreement at any time unless the parties have agreed on a period of notice, which shall not exceed 1 month. If agreed on in the credit agreement, the creditor may terminate the contract by giving the consumer at least 2 months' notice drawn up on paper or another durable medium. The creditor may also "for objectively justified reasons terminate the consumer's right to draw down on an open-end credit agreement", providing him/her with the reasons, again on paper or another durable medium.[52]

The right of withdrawal provides that the consumer has fourteen calendar days in which to withdraw from the credit agreement without having to give any reason. In order to exercise the right of withdrawal before the expiry of the 14 day deadline, the consumer must inform the creditor "by means which can be proven" and "pay to the creditor the capital and interest accrued thereon from the date the credit was drawn down until the capital is repaid without any undue delay and no longer than 30 calendar days after the despatch by him to the creditor of the notification of the withdrawal".[53] In the case of linked credit agreements, customer protection levels have been raised. In fact, article 15 provides that where the consumer has exercised a right of withdrawal, based on Community law, concerning a contract for the supply of goods or services, "he shall no longer be bound by the credit agreement". Furthermore, in the event of non-compliance, or partial or non-delivery of the goods covered by a linked credit agreement, the consumer "shall have the right to pursue remedies against the creditor if the consumer has pursued his remedies against the supplier but failed to obtain the satisfaction to which he is entitled". The same article also states it "shall be without prejudice to any national rules rendering the creditor jointly and severally liable in respect of any claim which the consumer may

---

[52]Article 13, subparagraph 2.

[53]Article 14, subparagraph 3, points (a) and (b).

5.5 Protection of Other Consumer Rights   115

Table 5.3 Differences between the first and the new Consumer Credit Directive: protection of other consumer rights

	Directive 87/102/EEC as amended	Directive 2008/48/EC
Open-end credit agreement	= = = = =	The consumer may effect standard termination of an open-end credit agreement free of charge at any time unless the parties have agreed on a period of notice that anyway may not exceed 1 month. If agreed in the credit agreement the creditor may effect standard termination of an open-end credit agreement by giving the consumer at least 2 months' notice. The creditor may also, for justified reasons, terminate the consumer's right to draw down on an open-end agreement (see article 13)
Right of withdrawal	= = = = =	The consumer shall have a period of 14 calendar days in which to withdraw from the credit agreement without giving any reason (see article 14) The article also indicates when that period of withdrawal shall begin and what the consumer has to do to exercise his right of withdrawal
Linked credit agreements	= = = = =	Where the consumer has exercised a right of withdrawal concerning a contract for the supply of goods and services he shall no longer be bound by a linked credit agreement (see article 15)
Early repayment	The consumer shall be entitled at any time to discharge his obligations under a credit agreement before the time fixed by the agreement. In this event the consumer shall be entitled to an equitable reduction in the total cost of the credit (see article 8)	The consumer shall be entitled at any time to discharge fully or partially his obligations under a credit agreement. In such cases, he shall be entitled to a reduction in the total cost of the credit, such reduction consisting of the interest and the costs for the remaining duration of the contract. In the event of early repayment of credit the creditor shall be entitled to fair and objectively justified compensation for possible costs directly linked to early repayment of credit (see article 16) The article specifies the maximum amount of the compensation and all cases when compensation for early repayment shall not be claimed
Assignment of rights	Where the creditor's rights under a credit agreement are assigned to a third person, the consumer shall be	In the event of assignment to a third party of the creditor's rights under a credit agreement the consumer shall be entitled to plead against the assignee any defence

(*continued*)

Table 5.3 (continued)

	Directive 87/102/EEC as amended	Directive 2008/48/EC
	entitled to plead against that third person any defence which was available to him against the original creditor (see article 9)	which was available to him against the original creditor. The consumer shall be informed of the assignment unless the original creditor continues to service the credit vis-à-vis the consumer (see article 17)
Overrunning	= = = = =	In the event of significant overrunning exceeding a period of 1 month the creditor shall inform the consumer without delay of the overrunning, the amount involved, the borrowing rate and any charges on arrears applicable (see article 18)

have against the supplier where the purchase of the goods or services from the supplier has been financed by a credit agreement".[54]

Although early repayment rights were already foreseen in the previous Directive, the new Directive lays down more precise guidelines. In the event of early repayment, whilst the first Directive foresaw an equitable reduction in the total cost of the credit, the new Directive states that the consumer "shall be entitled to a reduction in the total cost of the credit, such reduction consisting of the interest and the costs for the remaining duration of the contract." The interests of the creditor are also recognised, with the lender being entitled "to fair and objectively justified compensation for possible costs directly linked to early repayment". Compensation ceilings are fixed depending on the period of time between early repayment and the agreed termination of the credit agreement: no more than 1% of the amount of the credit repaid if repayment is made more than 1 year before the agreed termination date and no more than 0.5% of the amount of the credit repaid if repayment is made within 1 year of the agreed termination date.[55]

In the light of lenders' increasing recourse to securitisation and the resulting transfer to a third party of the creditor's rights under a credit agreement or the agreement itself, "the consumer shall be entitled to plead against the assignee any defence which was available to him against the original creditor" and shall be informed of the assignment except in the case where the original creditor, by agreement with the assignee, continues to service the credit vis-à-vis the consumer".[56]

Finally, in the case of overrunning, the consumer is protected essentially by informational rights.[57]

---

[54] Article 15, subparagraph 3.
[55] Article 16, subparagraphs 1 and 2.
[56] Article 17.
[57] Article 18.

As we have seen, many of the consumer rights provisions are already contained in national laws of major EU Member States. An interesting supplement to the Directive in this area is a 2 week extension granted in Germany in the event of a delay in payments to enable the consumer to make up the outstanding amount before the lender can exercise his right to terminate the agreement (*Verbraucherkreditgesetz*, Section 498 paragraph 1).

5.6 The Supervision of Creditors and Credit Intermediaries

Like the Directive that preceded it, the new Directive seeks to define a single regulatory framework for The Supervision of Creditors and Credit Intermediaries intermediaries. It does this by introduction simplifications, essentially establishing a principle and allowing individual Member States to choose the model for the supervision of financial institutions by independent bodies or authorities.

On the question of supervision, the first Directive already made a distinction between creditors (that is, consumer credit lenders), defined as "a natural or legal person who grants or promises to grant credit in the course of his trade, business or profession" and credit intermediaries (that is, consumer credit brokers), i.e. "a natural or legal person who is not acting as a creditor and who, in the course of his trade, business or profession, for a fee, which may take a pecuniary form or any other agreed form of financial consideration: (1) presents or offers credit agreements to consumers; (2) assists consumers by undertaking preparatory work in respect of credit agreements other than as referred to in (1); or (3) concludes credit agreements with consumers on behalf of the creditor". Despite the distinction made between the two types of intermediaries, as Table 5.4 shows, the first Directive grouped both together as regards authorisation, supervision and the handling of complaints.

The new Directive makes not only a terminological, but also a regulatory distinction between creditors on one hand and credit intermediaries on the other. As regards the former, Member States are given the opportunity to ensure that they are either supervised by an independent body or authority, or regulated,[58] whilst the second are no longer subject to regulation or supervision, but certain mandatory practices vis-à-vis consumers. Under the new Directive, Member States shall ensure that: a credit intermediary indicates in advertising and customer-directed documentation whether he works independently or with one or more creditors; the fee, if any, payable by the consumer to the credit intermediary is disclosed to the consumer; the fee, if any, payable by the consumer to the credit intermediary is communicated to the creditor by the credit intermediary for the purpose of calculation of APR.[59]

---

[58]Article 20 states that "This shall be without prejudice to Directive 2006/48/EC" relating to the possibility of offering banking services.

Table 5.4 Differences between the first and new Consumer Credit Directive: creditors and credit intermediaries

	Directive 87/102/EEC as amended	Directive 2008/48/EC
Creditors and credit intermediaries	Member States shall ensure that creditors or credit intermediaries: – Shall obtain official authorization to do so; or – Shall be subject to inspection or monitoring of their activities by an institution or official body; or – Promote the establishment of appropriate bodies to receive complaints (see article 12)	Member states shall ensure that creditors are supervised by a body or authority independent from financial institutions or regulated (see article 20) Member states shall ensure that a credit intermediary indicates the extent of his powers, in particular whether he works exclusively with one or more creditors or as an independent broker, and the fee payable by the consumer to the credit intermediary. Such a fee has to be communicated by the credit intermediary to the creditor for the purpose of calculation of APR (see article 21)

The changes introduced by the new Directive regarding the regulation and supervision of supply-side players provide a clearer European regulatory framework that matches more effectively lenders' and credit brokers' regulatory obligations with the need for solvency on one hand and best market practices on the other.

It is reasonable to suppose that the simplifications introduced by the new Directive are a pragmatic response to a particularly disparate European credit market scenario made up by different types of lenders authorised to grant credit or act as credit intermediaries.

In particular, whilst the conditions regulating lenders' access to and operations on the credit market are substantially similar in major EU countries, due to the fact that banks and financial institutions belong to the same industry and are subject to stringent levels of supervision, the same does not appear to apply to credit intermediaries, a category which, where present,[60] is characterised by cross-country differences in access to the profession and supervision of activities. These differences may regard the method of licensing, the possibility when necessary to suspend or strike off a person from the profession, and the disclosure of complaints.

With regards to lenders, most European countries traditionally restrict the activity of lending to universal banks and financial institutions. Universal banks are subject to the same regulation as the banking sector, in terms of authorisation, supervision and sanctions. Specialised consumer credit companies are, on the other hand, subject to specific, less stringent regulations in comparison to those applied to the banking industry as the range of activities they are authorised to offer is smaller than that supplied by universal banks. Such lenders are, however, subject to a

---

[60]These intermediaries are present in countries where the supply of consumer credit is restricted to banks and specialised finance companies. Their number is clearly much lower in those countries where credit can also be granted by licensed lenders who use funds from the banking system to finance specific market segments.

5.6 The Supervision of Creditors and Credit Intermediaries

blanket requirement in all legislations requiring them to be registered in a specific register. Moreover, they must possess minimum financial levels and be equipped with solid administrative, accounting and auditing procedures. Persons with administrative responsibilities within this category of lenders must also satisfy the requisites of integrity, professionalism and independence. National supervisory authorities are responsible for monitoring the activities of such credit companies and for ensuring compliance with national laws regulating consumer credit.

In some countries, consumer credit can also be offered by individuals, such as, in the United Kingdom, pawnbrokers or doorstep lenders,[61] with a consumer credit license issued by the office of fair trading (OFT). These lenders typically specialise in the sub-prime market, i.e. borrowers with difficulties in accessing credit from mainstream credit providers due to low incomes or previous episodes of default.

To do business, these lenders must satisfy a series of requisites established by the OFT – applicant's integrity,[62] credit competence,[63] credit risk profile of the business,[64] in addition to the presence of positive factors relevant to fitness[65] – not only to obtain a license, but also to keep it. Post-licensing supervision, in addition to ensuring the maintenance of standards, includes verifying compliance with regulations regarding advertising and contractual form and content. If a licensee fails to comply with the requirements or fails to provide relevant information to the OFT, the OFT has the power to impose financial penalties, and/or to revoke the licence or to take other licensing actions.

As mentioned above, cross-country differences exist as to the role and regulation of credit intermediaries.

In Italy, for instance, two types of credit intermediary exist: *Mediatori creditizi* (brokers) and *Agenti in attività finanziarie*.

---

[61] See Chap. 3, paragraph 2.

[62] Integrity issues are assessed by the OFT by evaluating the applicant's past behaviour as regards business behaviour and possible episodes of non-compliance with the law (i.e. criminal offenses involving violence, fraud, dishonesty, any breach of the Consumer Credit Act or of other consumer protection law or of rules or principles of the Financial Services Authority, insolvency bankruptcy or disqualification as a director, the provision of false or misleading information to the OFT).

[63] The credit competences required by the OFT relate to competence and experience in granting credit. In particular, with reference to the business activities that pose greater potential risks to consumers than others, such as secured sub-prime lending and lending in the home, the OFT applies for additional information about the business model and activities the applicant intends to follow in order to ensure that lending takes place responsibly (i.e. ability to check borrowers' creditworthiness).

[64] Authorisation is based on a risk assessment approach which implies the request of additional information, checks carried out on the applicant's premises and risk analyses of the business segment targeted by the applicant.

[65] For example, membership of an OFT-approved consumer code scheme or a record of fair dealing over a significant period (i.e. evidence of no serious consumer complaints or enforcement action taken against the applicant's business as well as an active policy of addressing consumer complaints).

Mediatori creditizi (regulated by Presidential decree (DPR) no. 28 of 28th July 2000) are identified as individuals who, in the course of their professional activities, offer brokerage services, on one hand, to banks and finance companies and, on the other, to potential borrowers. They operate independently from the parties involved and specialise in distributing loan requests signed by credit applicants.

Such brokers are required to be enrolled in a specific registry (*Albo dei mediatori creditizi*) subject to Bank of Italy authorisation following compliance with certain requirements, such as domicile in Italy, level of qualifications and professional and behavioural integrity as well as respect of legislation in the areas of information disclosure and money laundering.

Agenti in attività finanziarie are regulated by Ministerial decree (DM) 485/2001 and Legislative decree (d.lgs.) 374/1999. These professionals operate as agents on behalf of one or more financial intermediaries and offer the financial services foreseen by article 106 of the Consolidated Banking Law (*Testo Unico Bancario*). They have no powers in setting prices or establishing contractual conditions and are subject to the registration and operating requirements fixed for brokers.

In Spain, a bill introducing regulation of credit intermediaries along the same lines as brokers in Italy was presented as recently as July 2008. The bill seeks to regulate non financial entities that offer credit (*Entidades de mediacion de creditos*) which, though present on the Spanish market, are subject solely to the provisions of Spanish consumer law and not to regulations governing financial intermediaries or Bank of Spain supervision. The legislation proposes transparency and disclosure requirements along with registration (*Autoridades de consumo*) and oversight by the Bank of Spain.

In France, the Monetary and Financial Code Article L.519-1 regulates banking-transaction intermediaries (*Intermediarie en operations de banque*), i.e. any person who, in the normal course of his business and without being a del credere agent, effects introductions between parties interested in entering into a banking transaction. These professionals are subject to provisions relating to usury, money loans and advertising.

In Belgium, credit intermediaries are classified as either *Agent-délégué* or *Courtier de crédit*. Legislation in this area is more detailed than that currently in force in the countries referred to above. In fact, the Belgian *Code de la Consommation* (article 62, paragraphs 1 and 2), in seeking to promote responsible lending, states that these intermediaries shall not accept and therefore direct to lenders any loan applications by individuals who, on the basis of information provided, are likely to have difficulties in meeting repayment commitments. The legislation also provides that these intermediaries inform all the creditors they work for of any other applications received by the same consumer in the previous 2 months.

Credit intermediaries in Germany are subject to the provisions of article 655 a-e of the German Civil Code, which regulates, similarly to the new Directive, the economic conditions applied by these professionals. In particular, the contract between the intermediary and client must be in writing and must clearly state the commission payable calculated as a percentage of the total loan requested. This commission is payable only if the credit has been granted and the consumer can no longer invoke the right of withdrawal. The agreement must also mention the commission granted by the lender, where applicable. If the credit agreement is intended for the advanced repayment of another credit, the commission will be payable only if the APR, excluding the amount of the commission, of the new credit is not higher than that of the credit to be repaid and the intermediary was aware of the purpose.

5.7 Further Remarks

In addition to the considerations made in the previous paragraphs, attention needs to be drawn to two further aspects relating to the new Directive's contents. The first concerns to the scope of the Directive, whilst the second relates the out-of-court resolution of disputes.

As regards the scope of the Directive, its provisions apply in general to credit agreements. However, certain types of agreements are excluded from it.[66] Such

---

[66] The agreements excluded from the scope of the Directive are:

(a) credit agreements which are secured either by a mortgage or by another comparable security commonly used in a Member State on immovable property or secured by a right related to immovable property;

(b) credit agreements the purpose of which is to acquire or retain property rights in land or in an existing or projected building;

(c) credit agreements involving a total amount of credit less than EUR 200 or more than EUR 75,000;

(d) hiring or leasing agreements where an obligation to purchase the object of the agreement is not laid down either by the agreement itself or by any separate agreement; such an obligation shall be deemed to exist if it is so decided unilaterally by the creditor;

(e) credit agreements in the form of an overdraft facility and where the credit has to be repaid within 1 month;

(f) credit agreements where the credit is granted free of interest and without any other charges and credit agreements under the terms of which the credit has to be repaid within 3 months and only insignificant charges are payable;

(g) credit agreements where the credit is granted by an employer to his employees as a secondary activity free of interest or at annual percentage rates of charge lower than those prevailing on the market and which are not offered to the public generally;

(h) credit agreements which are concluded with investment firms as defined in Article 4(1) of Directive 2004/39/EC of the European Parliament and of the Council of 21st April 2004 on markets in financial instruments (1) or with credit institutions as defined in Article 4 of Directive 2006/48/EC for the purposes of allowing an investor to carry out a transaction relating to one or more of the instruments listed in Section C of Annex I to Directive 2004/39/EC, where the investment firm or credit institution granting the credit is involved in such transaction;

(i) credit agreements which are the outcome of a settlement reached in court or before another statutory authority;

(j) credit agreements which relate to the deferred payment, free of charge, of an existing debt;

(k) credit agreements upon the conclusion of which the consumer is requested to deposit an item as security in the creditor's safe-keeping and where the liability of the consumer is strictly limited to that pledged item;

exclusions appear justified both in economic and practical terms. Furthermore, the decision to recognise a substantial area of exclusion is in line with the full harmonisation principle[67] as it balances the need to extend the scope of application on one hand with the need to heighten the degree of harmonisation on the other.[68] In fact, in comparison to the first Directive, the number of exclusions has been raised, whilst at the same time increasing significantly the scope, with the inclusion of credit agreements under which the consumer is required to repay the credit either within a period not exceeding 3 months or by a maximum number of four payments within a period not exceeding 12 months. In this way, the new Directive captures new revolving forms of credit.

Importantly, the safeguard of higher levels of consumer protection foreseen in those countries with existing or planned further extensive consumer credit regulation is offered by the possibility of applying EU consumer credit regulations to other sectors provided such a choice is in compliance with EU law. Two examples are provided where a Member State could maintain or introduce national legislation which, though adopting all or only some of the provisions of the Directive, is applied to credit agreements outside its scope: credit agreements involving amounts less than Euro 200 or more than Euro 75,000 or linked credit agreements other than those defined in the Directive.[69]

With regards to the total amounts of credit covered by the Directive, the range from Euro 200 up to Euro 75,000 appears adequate and the decision to maintain a threshold is to be welcomed as this guarantees that minor bank account overdrafts and similar formulae which are simple to use and easy to repay continue to be excluded. The administrative overheads involved in granting small loans tend indeed to be high in relation to the earnings generated. As regards the Euro 75,000 ceiling, this was raised from the previous figure of Euro 20,000 so as to extend the benefits of transparency and cross-border competition to larger-sized loans. The Commission's decision to opt for a significantly higher ceiling is certainly bold as it challenges the relation that exists in theory between the total amount of a loan and the borrower's capacity to take care of himself also by seeking and obtaining expert advice.

(l) credit agreements which relate to loans granted to a restricted public under a statutory provision with a general interest purpose, and at lower interest rates than those prevailing on the market or free of interest or on other terms which are more favourable to the consumer than those prevailing on the market and at interest rates not higher than those prevailing on the market.

[67] See Sect. 5.2.

[68] Concerns regarding the difficulties this balancing act presents were expressed by the House of Lords (2006): "There is also a more general concern that the concept of full harmonisation is being expanded at the price of narrowing the field covered by the Directive".

[69] See Whereas (10).

5.7 Further Remarks

The second aspect regarding the Directive's contents is the importance given to out-of-court resolutions of consumer credit disputes.[70] In line with the aim of promoting the development of the internal market also by means of cross-border activities, Member States are asked to encourage cooperation between bodies responsible for the settlement of consumer disputes as a way of resolving cross-border consumer credit disputes. The objective here is to use wherever possible more flexible and user-friendly out-of-court solutions in preference to more complex and costly litigation procedures, especially when cross-border disputes are involved.

Priority to out-of-court settlement procedures not only reflects a general trend towards the use of these in consumer disputes, but is also consistent with the overarching aims of the Directive itself. In fact, out-of-court resolutions are a useful complement to the disclosure and transparency requirements set down by the Directive to provide a sufficient degree of consumer protection and confidence at all stages of the credit agreement.

Heightened levels of transparency should in fact favour the successful performance of consumer credit agreements and reduce the possibility of dispute. Additionally, more streamlined and flexible dispute resolution mechanisms will act as an effective deterrent to unfair behaviour on the part of lenders as consumers, who typically find litigation off-putting and complicated, will have greater incentives to protect their interests via out-of-court procedures.

Moreover, as seen previously concerning the question of the prevention and management of overindebtedness[71] and the increasing use of consumer credit amongst lower income and financially weaker households in general,[72] legislation that seeks to improve levels of transparency and customer protection must be flanked by parallel structures, such as debt counselling and financial literacy services, which seek to raise awareness amongst consumers of the financial implications of indebtedness.

---

[70] See article 24.
[71] See Chap. 4, paragraph 4.3.
[72] See Chap. 2, paragraph 2.3.

Appendix

Table 5.5 Reproduction of Annex II – "Standard European Consumer Credit Information", Official Journal of the European Union, 22.5.2008

1. Identity and contact details of the creditor/credit intermediary	
Creditor	[Identity]
Address	[Geographical address to be used by the consumer]
Telephone number[a]	
E-mail address[a]	
Fax number[a]	
Web address[a]	
If applicable	
Credit intermediary	[Identity]
Address	[Geographical address to be used by the consumer]
Telephone number[a]	
E-mail address[a]	
Fax number[a]	
Web address[a]	
2. Description of the main features of the credit product	
The type of credit	
The total amount of credit *This means the ceiling or the total sums made available under the credit agreement.*	
The conditions governing the drawdown *This means how and when you will obtain the money.*	
The duration of the credit agreement	
Instalments and, where appropriate, the order in which instalments will be allocated	You will have to pay the following: [The amount, number and frequency of payments to be made by the consumer] Interest and/or charges will be payable in the following manner:
The total amount you will have to pay *This means the amount of borrowed capital plus interest and possible costs related to your credit.*	[Sum of total amount of credit and total cost of credit]

(*continued*)

Appendix 125

Table 5.5 (continued)

If applicable The credit is granted in the form of a deferred payment for a good or service or is linked to the supply of specific goods or the provision of a service Name of good/service Cash price	
If applicable Sureties required *This is a description of the security to be provided by you in relation to the credit agreement.*	[Kind of sureties]
If applicable *Repayments do not give rise to immediate amortisation of the capital*	
3. Costs of the credit	
The borrowing rate or, if applicable, different borrowing rates which apply to the credit agreement	[% – fixed or, – variable (with the index or reference rate applicable to the initial borrowing rate), – periods],
APR *This is the total cost expressed as an annual percentage of the total amount of credit. The APR is there to help you compare different offers.*	[% A representative example mentioning all the assumptions used for calculating the rate to be set out here]
Is it compulsory, in order to obtain the credit or to obtain it on the terms and conditions marketed, to take out – an insurance policy securing the credit, or another ancillary service contract, – *If the costs of these services are not known by the creditor they are not included in the APR* Related costs	Yes/no [if yes, specify the kind of insurance] Yes/no [if yes, specify the kind of ancillary service]
If applicable Maintaining one or more accounts is required for recording both payment transactions and drawdowns	
If applicable Amount of costs for using a specific means of payment (i.e. a credit card)	
If applicable Any other costs deriving from the credit agreement	

(*continued*)

Table 5.5 (continued)

If applicable Conditions under which the abovementioned costs related to the credit agreement can be changed	
If applicable Obligation to pay notarial fees Costs in the case of late payments *Missing payments could have severe consequences for you (i.e. forced sale) and make obtaining credit more difficult.*	You will be charged [... (applicable interest rate and arrangements for its adjustment and, where applicable, default charges)] for missing payments.
4. Other important legal aspects	
Right of withdrawal *You have the right to withdraw from the credit agreement within a period of 14 calendar days.* Early repayment *You have the right to repay the credit early at any time in full or partially*	Yes/no
If applicable The creditor is entitled to compensation in the case of early repayment	[Determination of the compensation (calculation method) in accordance with the provisions implementing Article 16 of Directive 2008/48/EC]
Consultation of a database *The creditor must inform you immediately and without charge of the result of a consultation of a database, if a credit application is rejected on the basis of such a consultation. This does not apply if the provision of such information is prohibited by European Community law or is contrary to objectives of public policy or public security.* Right to a draft credit agreement *You have the right, upon request, to obtain a copy of the draft credit agreement free of charge. This provision does not apply if the creditor is at the time of the request unwilling to proceed to the conclusion of the credit agreement with you.*	
If applicable The period of time during which the creditor is bound by the pre-contractual information	This information is valid from ... until ...

(continued)

Appendix 127

Table 5.5 (continued)

5. Additional information in the case of distance marketing of financial services

(a) concerning the creditor

If applicable Representative of the creditor in your Member State of residence Address Telephone number[a] E-mail address[a] Fax number[a] Web address[a]	[Identity] [Geographical address to be used by the consumer]
If applicable Registration	[The trade register in which the creditor is entered and his registration number or an equivalent means of identification in that register]
If applicable The supervisory authority	

(b) concerning the credit agreement

If applicable Exercise of the right of withdrawal	[Practical instructions for exercising the right of withdrawal indicating, inter alia, the period for exercising the right, the address to which notification of exercise of the right of withdrawal should be sent and the consequences of non-exercise of that right]
If applicable The law taken by the creditor as a basis for the establishment of relations with you before the conclusion of the credit contract	
If applicable Clause stipulating the governing law applicable to the credit agreement and/or the competent court	[Relevant clause to be set out here]
If applicable Language regime	Information and contractual terms will be supplied in [specific language]. With your consent, we intend to communicate in [specific language/languages] during the duration of the credit agreement.

(c) concerning redress

Existence of and access to out-of-court complaint and redress mechanism	[Whether or not there is an out-of-court complaint and redress mechanism for the consumer who is party to the distance contract and, if so, the methods of access to it]

[a]This information is optional for the creditor

Wherever "if applicable" is indicated, the creditor must fill in the box if the information is relevant to the credit product or delete the respective information or the entire row if the information is not relevant for the type of credit considered

Indications between square brackets provide explanations for the creditor and must be replaced with the corresponding information

References

Alessie R, Devereux MP, Weber G (1997) Intertemporal consumption, durables and liquidity constraints: a cohort analysis. Eur Econ Rev 41:1

Anderloni L (1997) Il sovraindebitamento in Italia e in Europa. In:Ruozi R (ed) L'usura in Italia, Egea, Milano

Anderloni L, Braga D, Carluccio E (2006) New frontiers in Banking services. Emerging needs and taylored products for untapped market. Springer, Berlin

Ando A, Modigliani F (1957) Tests of the life-cycle hypothesis of savings: comments and suggestions. Bull Oxf Inst Stat 19:99–124

ASF (2007) Annual Report – Association Francaise des Sociétés Financieres. Juin

ASSOFIN (2007), Osservatorio sul credito al dettaglio, Research Report n.23, Milan

Athanasoglou PP, Brissimis SN, Delis MD (2005) Bank-specific, industry-specific and macroeconomic determinants of bank profitability, Bank of Greece, Working paper, n.25

Attanasio O (1999) Consumption. In: Taylor JB, Woodford M (eds) Handbook of macroeconomics, Elsevier, Amsterdam

Bagliano FC, Bertola G (2004) Models for dynamic macroeconomics. Oxford University, Oxford

Banco de Espana (2007) Boletin economico.07–08

Banco de Espana Encuesta financiera de las familias (EFF), various years

Bank of Italy (2006) Annual report

Bank of Italy Survey of household income and wealth (SHIW), various years

Bank of Spain (2004) Annual report

Bank of France, (2003) Consumer credit, Research report

Banque de France (1996) Traitement du surendettement: nouvelles perspectives, bulletin 2 trimestre, Supplement Etudes

Banque de France (2004) Revue de la stabilité financière, June

Banque de France (2005) Enquête typologique 2004 sur le surendettement, February

Banque Nationale de Belgique (2004) Annual report

Bianco M, Jappelli T, Pagano M (2002) Courts and banks: effects of judicial enforcement on credit markets, CSEF – Centre for studies in economics and finance, Working paper, n.58

Bicakova A (2007) Does the good matter? evidence on moral hazard and adverse selection from consumer credit market, European University Institute, Economics Working paper, n.2

BITE (2006) La demande des ménages en matière de credit à la consummation et les ajustements necessaries pour y répondre, January

Boudasse T, Lavigne A (2000), Pourquoi et comment legiférer sur l'usure Revue d'Economie Financère

Bridges S, Disney R (2004) Use of credit and arrears on debt among low-income families in the United Kingdom. Fiscal Stud 25:1

Brown S., Taylor K, Wheatley Price S. (2005) Debt and distress: evaluating the psychological cost of credit. J Econ Psychol 26:642–663

Bulgarian National Bank (2007), Household behaviour, Economic review, n.3

Caskey J (1994) Fringe banking. Russell Sage Foundation, New York

Casolaro L, Gambacorta L, Guiso L (2006) Regulation, formal and informal enforcement and the development of the household loan market. Lesson from Italy. In: Bertola G, Disney R, Grant C (eds) The economics of consumer credit, MIT, Massachusetts

Cavalletti B, Lagazio C, Vandone D (2008) Il credito al consumo in Italia: benessere economico o fragilità finanziaria? Università di Milano, DEAS working paper, n.24

CEACCU (2007) Guia Pratica: sovreendeudamiento familiar, como evitarlo? www.ceaccu.es

CGAP (2004) The impact of interest rate ceilings on microfinance. Consultative Group to Assist the Poor, Washington, p18

Chandler G, Parker L (1989) Predictive value of credit bureau reports. J Retail Bank 11:4

Competition Commission (2008) Market investigation into payment protection insurance, June

Consumer Affairs Victoria (2006) The report of the consumer credit review. Consumer Affairs Victoria

Consumer and financial literacy task force (2004) Australian consumer and money, Discussion paper

Costa CA, Pinto L (2005) Sobre-endividamento dos consumidores no concelho da Trofa, Núcleo de Investigação em Microeconomia Aplicada, Braga

Crook J (2003) The demand and supply for household debt: a cross country comparison, University of Edinburgh, Credit research Centre, Working paper

Crook J (2005) The measurement of household liabilities: conceptual issues and practices, University of Edinburgh, Credit research Centre, Working paper

Crook J (2006), Household Debt Demand and Supply. In: Bertola G, Disney R, Grant C (eds) The economics of consumer credit, MIT, Massachusetts

Crook J, Edelman D, Thomas L (2007) Recent development in consumer credit risk assessment, European Journal Operation Research

Crook J, Hochguertel S (2007) US and European household debt and credit constraints: comparative micro evidence from the last 15 years, Tinbergen Institute, Discussion paper, 07/3

Cox D, Jappelli T (1993) The effect of borrowing constraints on consumer liabilities. J Money Credit Bank 25:2

Davydoff D, Naacke G (2005) L'endettement des ménages européens, Report achieved by the Observatoire de l'Epargne Européenne for the Comité Consultatif du Secteur Financier

Deaton A (1992) Understanding consumption. Oxford University, Oxford

Del Rio A, Young G (2005a) The determinants of unsecured borrowing: evidence from the British Household Panel Survey, Bank of England, Working paper n 263

Del Rio A, Young G (2005b) The impacts of unsecured debt among British households, Bank of England, working paper, n.262

Diez Guardia N. (2002) Consumer credit in the European Union, ECRI research report, n.1, CEPS, Brussels, February

Dominy N, Kempson E (2003), Pay day advances - the companies and their customers, Research Report, The Personal Finance Research Centre, University of Bristol

DTI (2000) Report on costs and interest rates in the small loans sector. London

DTI (2003) White paper: Fair, clear and competitive: the consumer credit market in the 21st century. London

DTI-MORI (2005) Over-indebtedness in Britain: A DTI report on the MORI Financial Services survey 2004. London

Duygan B, Grant C (2008) Household debt repayment behaviour: what role do institutions play?, FRB of Boston Quantitative Analysis Unit, Working paper, n.3

Elliott, A (2005) Not waving but drowning: Over-indebtedness by misjudgement. CSFI, London

EPC (2006) SEPA Card Framework. Version 2.0

European Central Bank (2005) Annual Report

References

European Central Bank (2006) Annual Report
European Commission (2005) Discussion paper on consumer credit, Health and consumer protection directorate-general
European Financial Services Round Table (2006) Consumer protection, consumer choice, Report, January
Fabbri D, Padula M (2004) Do poor legal enforcement make households credit constrained? J Bank Finance 28
Farinha L (2004) Households' debt burden: an analysis based on microeconomic data, Banco de Portugal, Economic Bulletin, September
Fay S, Hurst E, White M (2002) The household bankruptcy decision. Am Econ Rev 92:3
Fernando NA (2006) Understanding and dealing with high interest rates on microcredit, Asian Development Bank
Ferri G, Simon P (2000) Constrained consumer lending: methods using the survey of consumer finances, Università di Bari, Working paper, October
Filotto U (1999) Manuale del credito al consumo. Egea, Milano
Filotto U, Nicolini G (2007), Credito alla famiglia e consapevolezza dei consumatori. Una proposta operative. In: Bracchi G, Masciandaro D (eds) XII Rapporto sul sistema finanziario italiano. Banche italiane: una industria al bivio. Mercati, consumatori, governance. Edibank
Frade K (2004) The fable of the grasshopper and the ant: a research project on over-indebtedness and unemployment in Portugal. University of Coimbra, Coimbra
Freixas X, Rochet JC (1997) Economic Bancaria, Antoni Bosch Editor
Friedman M (1957) The permanent Income Hypothesis: comment. Am Econ Rev 48
FSA (2005) Measuring financial capability: an explanatory study, n.37, June
FSA (2006) Levels of financial capability in the UK: results of a baseline survey, n.47, March
GAO (2006) Financial literacy and education commission, US Government Accountability Office, Report to congressional committees, December
Gloukoviezoff, G (2006) Surendettement des particuliers en France. International Labour Office, Geneva
Graham F, Isaac AG. (2002) The behavioural life-cycle theory of consumer behaviour: survey evidence. J Econ Behav Organ 48
Grant C (2003) Estimating credit constraints among US households, European University Institute, Working paper, Florence
Grant C, Padula M (2006) Informal credit markets, judicial costs and consumer credit: evidence from firm level data, CSEF – Centre for Studies in Economics and Finance, Working paper, n.155
Grant C., Padula M (2007) Bounds repayment behaviour: evidence for the consumer credit market, Cà Foscari Università di Venezia, Working paper Department of Economics, p 26
Gropp R, Scholz JK, White MJ (1997) Personal Bankruptcy and credit supply and demand. Q J Econ 112
Guiso L, Sapienza P, Zingales P (2004) Does financial development matter? Q J Econ 119:3
Haas O (2006) Overindebtedness in Germany, Employment Sector International Labour Office Geneva, working paper, n.44
Hathaway I, Khatiwada S (2008) Do financial education programs work? FRB of Cleveland, Working paper, n.3
House of Lords (2006) Consumer credit in the European Union: harmonisation and consumer protection, Report, vol. I, July
International Monetary Fund (2006) Greece: Financial System Stability Assessment, n.6, January
Jappelli T, Pagano M (1993), Information sharing in credit markets, Journal of Finance, vol. 48 n.5
Jappelli T, (2005) The life-cycle hypothesis, fiscal policy and social security, CSEF – Centre for Studies in Economics and Finance, Working paper, n.40
Jappelli T, Pagano M (2002) Information sharing, lending and defaults: cross-country evidence in J Bank Finance, p 10

Jappelli T, Pagano M (2006) The role and effects of credit information sharing. In: Bertola G, Disney R, Grant C (eds) The economics of consumer credit, MIT, Massachusetts

Johansson MW, Persson M, Swedish households' indebtedness and ability to pay – a household level study, Penning Och Valutapolitik

Johnson RW, Johnson DP (1998) Pawnbroking in the US: a profile of customers. Credit Research Center, West Lafayette

Johnson RW, Sullivan AC (1983) Restrictive effects of rate ceilings on consumer choice. Credit Research Center, West Lafayette

Karlsson N, Dellgran P, Klingander B, Garlin T (2004) Household consumption: influences of aspiration level, social comparison and money management. J Econ Psychol p 25

Kempson E (2002) Over-indebtedness in Britain. Department of Trade and Industry, London

Kempson E (2008) Looking beyond our shores: consumer protection regulation lessons from the UK, Joint Center for Housing Studies of Harvard, February

Kilborn J (2005) Behavioural economics, overindebtedness and comparative consumer bankruptcy: searching for causes and evaluating solutions. Bankruptcy Dev J 22

Kish A (2006) Perspectives on recent trends in consumer debt, Federal Reserve Bank of Philadelphia, Discussion paper, June

Koljonen V, Romer-Paakkanen T (2000) Overindebtedness from the viewpoint of young debtor, County Administrative Board of Southern Finland Publications

Korczak D (2000) Over-indebtedness in Germany at the edge of 21st century, Money Matters No.3/00

Lea S, Webley P, Walker C (1995) Psychological factors in consumer debt: money management, economic socialization and credit use. J Econ Psychol 16

Le Duigou JP (2000) Endettement et surendettement des menages, Conseil Economique et Social, Paris

Magri S (2002) Italian households' debt: determinant of demand and supply, Banca d'Italia, Temi di discussione, p 454

Magri S (2007) Italian households' debt: the participation to the debt market and the size of the loan. Empirical Economics, Springer.vol. 33 p 3, November

May O, Tudela M, Young G (2004) British Household indebtedness and financial stress: a household-level picture, Bank of England, Quarterly Bulletin, Winter

Meier S, Sprenger C (2007) Impatience and credit behaviour: evidence from a field experiment, Centre for Behavioral Economics and Decision Making, Federal Reserve Bank of Boston

Miller MJ (2005) Credit reporting systems and the international economy. MIT, Cambridge

Modigliani F, Brumberg R (1954), Utility analysis and the consumption function: an interpretation of cross-section data. In: Kurihana K (ed) PostKeynesian economics, Rutgers University, New Brunswick

Modigliani F, Jappelli T, Pagano M (1985) The impact of fiscal policy and inflation on National saving: the Italian case, Banca Nazionale del Lavoro, Quarterly Review, p 153

Modigliani F (1988) The role of intergenerational transfers and life cycle saving in the accumulation of wealth. J Econ Perspect 2

Molyneux P (2006) What are the specific economic gains from improved financial inclusion? A tentative for estimating these gains. In: Anderloni L, Braga D, Carluccio E (eds) New frontiers in banking services. Emerging needs and taylored products for untapped market, Springer, Berlin

Nielsen AC, Anz (2005) ANZ Survey of adult financial literacy in Australia, November

Niemi-Kieslainen J, Henrikson AS (2005) Report on legal solutions to debt problems in credit societies, Bureau on the European Commettee on Legal Co-Operation (CDCJ-BU), October

Nieto F (2007) The determinant of household credit in Spain, Banco de Espana, Working paper, n.0716

Observatoire du Crédit et de l'endettement (2005) Rapport général sur la consommation et le crédit aux particulier, Paris

References

Observatorio do Endividamento (2002) Sobreendividamento, un estudo de caso, Relatorio de actividades 2002

OCR Macro (2001) Study of the problem of Consumer Indebtedness: Statistical aspects, Final Report submitted to Commission of the EU DG for Health and Consumer Protection

OECD (2005) Improving Financial Literacy. Analysis of issues and policies. OECD Publishing

OEE (2004) L'endettement des ménages européens de 1995 à 2002, April

OEE (2005) L'endettement des ménages européens, August

OEE, CESP, CRPF (2007) Towards a common operational European definition of over-indebtedness, Final Report submitted to Commission of the EU DG Employment, Social Affairs and Equal Opportunities

Ossfin (2007) Osservatorio sugli intermediari finanziari specializzati nel leasing, factoring e credito al consumo, Rapporto annuale

Oxera (2003) Assessment of the economic impact of the proposed EC consumer credit directive, Report, Oxford Economic Research Associates, England, July

Oxera (2007) The benefits of financial regulation: what to measure and how? Report prepared for the Financial Services Authority, Oxford Economic Research Associates, England

Payne J, Callender C (1997) Student loans: who borrows and why? Policy Studies Institute

PFRC (2006) Illegal lending in the Uk Research report, November

Poppe C (2008) Into the debt quagmire. How defaulters cope with severe debt problems, University of Oslo, Department of Sociology and Human Geography, Series of Dissertations, n.124

Ranyard R, Hinkley L, Williamson J, McHugh S (2006) The role of mental accounting in consumer credit decision processes. Journal of Economic Psychology.27:4

Reifner U, Kiesilainen J, Huls N, Springeneer H (2003) Consumer overindebtedness and consumer law in the European Union, Final Report submitted to Commission of the EU DG for Health and Consumer Protection

Reifner U, Knobloch M, Laatz W, Cantow M (2007) Iff uberschuldungsreport 2007, Private uberschuldung in Deutschland

Rinaldi L, Sanchez-Arellano A (2006) Household debt sustainability. What explains household non-performing loans? An empirical analysis, European Central Bank, Working paper, n.570

Rowlingson K, Kempson E (1993) Gas debt and disconnections. Policy Studies Institute, London

Salmi J (2000) Student loans in international perspective: The World Bank Experience, LCSHD Paper Series

Saunders A, Cornett MM (2007) Financial markets and institutions. An introduction to the risk management approach. The McGraw hill Companies, third edition

Skiba PM, Tobacman J (2008) Do payday loans cause bankruptcy? Working paper, February

Staten ME, Johnson, RW (1995) The case for deregulating interest rates on consumer credit. Purdue University, Credit Research Center, West Lafayette

Stiglitz J, Weiss A (1981) Credit rationing in markets with imperfect information. American Economic Review.71:3

Stone B, Vasquez Maury R (2006) Indicators of personal financial debt using a multi-disciplinary behavioural model. J Econ Psychol 27:4

Sveriges Konsumentrad (2006) Modified proposal for a new Directive on Consumer Credit, Position paper, January

Supriya S, McKeown W, Myers P, Shelly M (2005) Literature review on personal credit and debt, RMIT University, Working paper

Tardieu L (2007) Informal sources of credit and the Soft information market, Bulgarian National Bank, Discussion paper, n.58

Tatom J, Godstead D (2006) Targeting the unbanked-financial literacy's magin bullet?, University Library of Munich, MPRA paper 4266, Germany

Thomas LC, Edelman DB, Crook JN (2002) Credit scoring and its applications, Society for Industrial and applied Mathematics SIAM, Philadelphia

Uk Data Archive, British household panel survey (BHPS), various years

Vandone D (2001) L'intervento delle banche italiane nel mercato delle carte di pagamento. Edizioni ISU, Milano

Vandone D, Anderloni L (2008) Households over-indebtedness in the economic literature, University of Milan, Working paper, 46, December

Valkama E (2004), The effects of the Act on economic and debt councelling in the early 21st century, Research Report, Helsinki

Vercammen (1995) Credit bureau policy and sustainable reputation effects in credit markets. Economica.n.62

Villegas, DJ (1989) The impact of usury ceilings on consumer credit. Southern Economic Journal.56

Waldron M, Young G (2006) The state of British household finances: results from the 2006 NMG research survey, Bank of England Quarterly Bulletin, Q4

Watson J (2003) The relationship of materialism to spending tendencies, saving and debt. J Econ Psychol 24

Weill L (2004) Efficiency of Consumer Credit Companies in the European Union. A Cross-country Frontier Analysis, ECRI Research Report No. 7

Willis L (2008a) Evidence and Ideology in assessing the effectiveness of financial literacy education, University of Pennsylvania Law School, Research paper, n.8

Willis L (2008b) Against financial literacy education, University of Pennsylvania Law School, Research paper, n.10

World Bank (2005) Indicators of financial access – Households. Level Surveys

Yang S, Markoczy L, Qi M (2007) Unrealistic optimism in consumer credit card adoption. J Econ Psychol 28

Ziederman A. (2002) Alternative Objective of National Student Loan Schemes: implication for design, evaluation and policy. Welsh J Educ 1:1